"Rod Tafoya's autobiography"

AGELESS ARM

...My passion lives in the core!

Rod Tafoya

Edited by
Arnie Leshin

SPEAKING VOLUMES, LLC

NAPLES, FLORIDA

2012

AGELESS ARM

ISBN 978-1-61232-581-1

For

Maude and **Tony**, my beloved parents, who gave me my work ethic, while instilling the gift of passion and will to dream big. Thank you for your unconditional love, spirit and torch of inspiration.

To my brother, **Jack**, for your motivation, encouragement and vision to see what no one else thought possible. Thank you for your endearing dedication and life-long support.

Photograph by Nick Sedillos

Arnie Leshin's
Intro to the AGELESS ARM

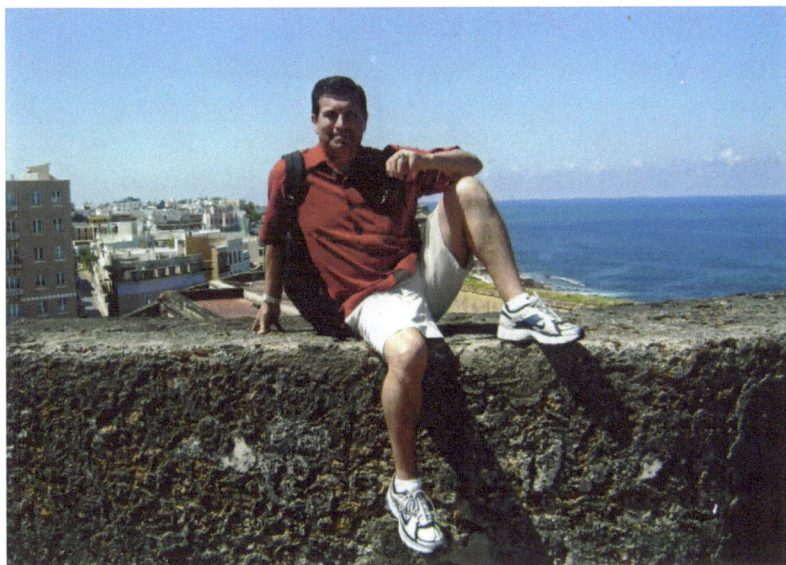

It was late at night when I received the call. It was 'so' late, that I was fast asleep.

When I checked my voice messages the next day, I learned who it was, the man with the (left) arm that he never puts to sleep. The ageless wonder of the hill, the traveling man calling to inform me of his latest adventures on the mound.

He was calling from Puerto Rico, saying this was just a brief on what he accomplished in the 15th annual Men's Senior Baseball League Winter Championships. In a span of six hours at the ballpark in Gurabo, he toiled 15 innings and threw 222 pitches in a doubleheader. He allowed nine hits and struck out 14 in the back-to-back games.

Knowing Rod Tafoya, I wasn't surprised, just amazed. But I love to hear it.

I'm thinking that it was neat to show his skills in yet another land, that this is a guy who was approaching 45. Yet, to him, age is just a number as he rubs up the ball, grips the stitching, rears back, and throws.

As he says, his *"Passion lives in the core"*.

And if you think his arm is weary, check with the batters having to deal with the 'heat' he fires, which blended in this time with the warm weather in Puerto Rico.

When he returned to Santa Fe, he filled me in.

He said that after pitching the first game of the twin bill, he intentionally left his glove and spikes in the car because he didn't think they would have him throw the next game. That he had downed a couple pieces of chicken along with a barbeque sandwich. That he had already 'iced' up his shoulder and pitching elbow.

Surprise.

His team, the Legends, relied on him to pitch the opener, but now they needed to win the closer to gain the title game, so why not bring back the best you have?

So, with a shrug of his shoulders, back to the hill he went, taking his left arm and passion for the game along. By the eighth inning, he was spent, pale, and dehydrated. He was feeling queasy and nauseated. By that time, his team was ahead 9-3 and he managed to hang in there.

His job now done, Tafoya was able to look on and cheer as the Legends took care of the Daytona Beach Rangers, 6-3, in the championship game played in

Caguas. Afterward, he was clutching the Most Valuable Player trophy in his non-pitching arm.

Yet another championship for him to add to his list.

Now, as his story is told in his autobiography, he simply grew up with the game. At the age of two, his brother Jack switched him from a righty to a lefty, which followed with a non-stop journey as a southpaw.

The road included Little League, recreation leagues, high school, college, amateur leagues, semi-pro, professional ball, travels to not only Puerto Rico, but to Mexico, Canada, and about a dozen or two other states, east, west, north and south of Santa Fe, his hometown.

Is he on some kind of mission? Well, consider the fact that he has already put up remarkable numbers ... No-hitters, one-hitters, shutouts, strikeouts, and few walks. Then there's the number 260. That's how many victories he has though the years. He would like to reach 300, and who can doubt him?

When I was first informed about Rod Tafoya and all his baseball heroics, I listened. When I made a visit to this home, I learned.

Now I've been a sports journalist for five decades, and I have my walls and desks dressed up with media credentials, awards, newspaper clips, autographed books, and whatever else I've saved through the many years.

But Rod is baseball and he has this one room packed neatly with more baseballs than I've ever seen. The room is neatly organized, with about 500 souvenir baseballs that highlight his years on the mound, from the past to the present.

There are also autographed balls from major league Hall of Fame players, coaches, teammates, all resting in this designated room of bats, caps, uniforms, trophies, and other memorabilia's.

No doubt I was impressed. Anyone would be. It's a treasure chest so cool, he could actually hold tours.

He's the traveling man with the magic arm, also employed as a vice president of the *Bank of the West* in Albuquerque, New Mexico.

At his alma mater —St. Michael's High School in Santa Fe—he has answered the call over the last 15 years to provide batting practice for the teams. He finds time to provide youngsters with the mechanics of pitching.

I have trouble keeping up with him. He makes stops wherever there's a request for his arm or as he says, "An arm for hire." He's a known quantity, well respected. Name a league and he's already pitched for it. No matter if it's 18-and-under or 40-and-over, he's the master of the hill.

And it shows on his license plate that spells out ACE-LHP.

How proud he is as he grinds along, feeling good about his drive to win 300, feeling more athletic and optimistic each time out.

Yes, age is just a number for him, something like the different ones he wears on his uniform. He runs about 45 miles a week. He works on the treadmills. He ran his first marathon—at Disney World—and turned in a 3:54 over the 26 miles, 385 yards. He said 18,000 started, 12,000 finished, and that he was proud to cross the finish line.

At 5-foot-10, 160 pounds, he works to keep his body in tune, noting that he lost 30 pounds prepping for the marathon, and feels even better because of this.

He's thinking 300 wins in maybe three-four years. He's thinking he can achieve this by pitching 18-19 times each season, which, in his case, includes both summer and winter. At one time last year, he was on the roster of seven different teams.

It's like this: If there's a baseball game to be played, he's available. His strength is his fastball. He's still throwing 86-87 miles per hour. He shows a curve, but it's his slider that he considers nasty.

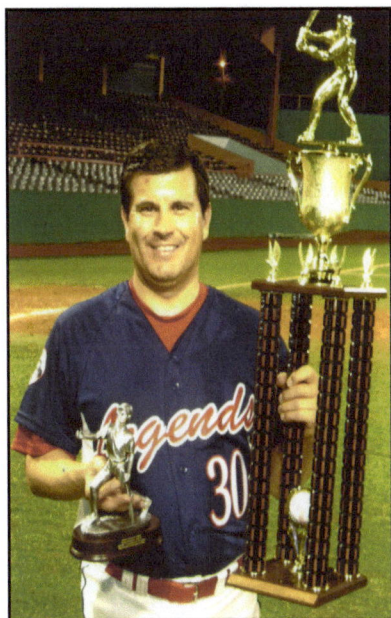

No, baseball never gets old for Rod Tafoya—the ball, the glove, the game.

And if you know the way to Santa Fe, check him out, but not from the batter's box.

As for the **AGELESS ARM**, once you begin following it chapter by chapter, you will marvel at what it brings to these pages. It's entertaining, interesting, lively ... a book for all ages.

Note: *ARNIE LESHIN is the author of several books—Including "The Best Damn Sports Stories"! He is in his sixth decade as a journalist. He has covered high schools, colleges and professional sports. He has covered World Series, Super Bowls, Stanley Cups, Olympics and the college basketball Final Four.*

Photograph by Nick Sedillos

A "TRIPP" BACK IN TIME BEFORE TURNING THE PAGES

Gary Tripp served as executive director of the New Mexico Activities Association since 2004. Back in his days at New Mexico Highlands University, he was team captain and leading hitter on its baseball team. He had no problem recalling former teammate Rod Tafoya.

He was a little lefty with a big fastball.

He was like a little bull, did not back down to anybody.

He had a great attitude, just wanted to take the mound and play the game, so it was easy to see how much he loved baseball.

He always looked to be on a mission to be successful, so I'm not surprised at what he has accomplished.

He is still pitching at the age of 47, and that's remarkable. Not only that, but he's winning, still throwing that fastball past batters.

He just reared back and battled. It didn't matter who he was playing against. I remember hitting a home run to win the game for Rod against Denver University. He was a freshman and our hottest pitcher. He started games, he relieved. I believe he made All-Conference.

I saw him play at St. Michael's High School (Santa Fe) and he was also quite the hitter. He wasn't as good at the college level, but he sure would battle when he batted.

A great kid then. A great man now. I'm happy to have learned about the success he has achieved through the years.

I'm looking forward to getting together with him. That would be a blast. And yes, I can hardly wait to read his book.

—GARY TRIPP

THE LINEUP

TURNING THINGS AROUND
Ages 2-6

It all began in Santa Fe, New Mexico. That's where I was born and raised.

When I reached the age of two, I looked up to my brother Jack. Not because he was much taller, but because he was 15 years older. There wasn't anything I could teach him, so when he talked, I listened.

And if he had an idea, I thought it was great. Like I said, I was only two. I knew I had two arms and couldn't question Jack when he decided to tie my right arm behind my back.

To me, it was a game, and at my age, I loved games. But what Jack had in mind was not as much as game as it was a strategy.

Little did he know he was preparing his little brother for a baseball career as a left-hander. Little did he know his little brother would be throwing a baseball from the left side until he was, let's say, 50,

or as I reached the standard retirement age of 65, I was still toiling on the mound.

Yes, I was born to use my right hand, but Jack had other ideas.

It involved more than pitching, for Jack thought in baseball it was quicker for a left-handed batter to run to first base. He thought lefties were also known as good hitters. He thought that lefty pitchers had a natural curveball.

Whatever he might have thought, I was still two years old.

And so it was Jack's high school days, while my parents were away on vacation in the Bahamas, that he and my brother, Glenn, decided to have a party. They invited classmates. They partied while little brother walked around with his right arm tied around his back.

Almost two years later, Jack went off to college, where he asked the advice of a professor, inquiring whether changing little young me would have any ramifications in the future. All this time, Jack had 'left brain,' 'right brain,' on his mind.

At which the professor informed him that because I was now approaching four, my brain was already making a choice to become a left-hander. Hearing that, Jack then instructed my parents that I was always to use my left hand for eating, writing, and especially for throwing.

Each time he returned home, we would play catch for hours. When he returned to college, Glenn and my mom took turns playing catch with me in the back yard. On one occasion, my dad showed up with a new catcher's mitt.

Within five minutes of our catch, my dad threw a hard one that sailed past my glove and landed in my chest. When it hit me, we both just looked at each other in silence. Then I called my dad a name that was off base for a now 5-year-old. That was it for my dad. He called it a career of playing catch with me, although he would go on to lend his support when I played on teams.

But Jack never quit on me. He was often joined by my sister Judy's ex-husband, Leonard. One time we were playing catch for about two hours and Leonard said he was tired, that it was time to quit. I ran into my house, went to my mom and began to cry because Leonard stopped playing catch with me. I remember Leonard saying that I was fascinated with baseball.

And my dad, well, while only being a little leaguer, to him I was spending too much time playing baseball. Playing from sun up to sundown was a little much for him. He thought that I had better things to do with my time, like learn in school and get an education.

My dad, Tony, was employed in Los Alamos at the Scientific Laboratory, where he worked in a tool plant. He had worked his way up to eighth grade in school before his education was done. In later years, with a family of five, he worked hard to provide for our family. His main concerns in life were for his children to get an education and have successful careers.

Rod Tafoya and Gabriel Martinez

As for myself, I was growing up with baseball on my mind.

At 6 years old, I played on my first organized team. We were the Capital City Plumbing. We wore orange tee shirts with the name of the team in black letters across my chest. We wore white pants with a black belt.

It was in the summer of the next season where I began to excel in baseball. I now played for Richard Peck Construction. I now wore a white with red pinstriped uniform with a bright red cap that read RP. The coach was Tommy Alvarez, the neighborhood mailman.

What was great being with Peck Construction was that we played on the field that was my recess playground during the day at Gonzales Elementary, and I felt right at home. While on that same playground in fifth grade, I was awarded the white ribbon for third longest throw during our Sports Events Day.

It was then that I realized that I had a chance to do something as a baseball player. Thanks to Jack, I was a left-hander for life.

THE BALL WAS IN MY HANDS
Ages 11-12

Of course my classmates and I weren't on the same base paths. It was in Mrs. Fleming's fifth grade class when one of them brought a Ouija board to class. As each student had a turn, they were asked a question, the pendulum would swing, and wherever it landed was the answer to your question.

As my turn came, I had an obvious question to ask, that being "Will I be a professional baseball player?" I vividly recall all of the class laughing at me. But, who cared, for baseball was all I thought about, talked about. Heck, I even dreamed baseball.

And so I thought, one day I'll have the last laugh. As sure as there are stitches in the baseball, I'm going to make it and no one is going to stop me, not even my dad.

By the time I reached the sixth grade at age 12, I had worked my way up to Little League ball. I was an All-Star pitcher in what was called the Metropolitan Little League. I was one of the fastest pitchers in the league. Not a-foot, but by way of my southpaw arm.

Being selected to the LL All-Star team was my finest accomplishment. Even my family was proud, especially my dad. He would attend all of my games and talk with his buddies about how fast I was throwing the ball.

"He's a small kid," I remember him saying, "but his mechanics allow him to throw faster than all the other kids."

Of course, those were the same mechanics that Jack taught me in the back yard. There were endless hours of repetition. Bro Jack made me a perfectionist on the mound. There was certainly room for error, and when there was, we did it all over again until I got it right.

Little League baseball All-Star practice was underway and lucky for me it was right across the Santa Fe River and a five-minute quickie from my house to Alto Park.

We had the three best pitchers in the league. There was Frank Casados from McDonald's, Joe Pat Romero from Dial Finance, and myself from 3BR & Construction. Casados and Romero had stronger arms than I did, which is why they placed first and second in the fifth grade baseball toss the year before.

After weeks of early morning practices and final cuts, our team was ready for its first game. We played game one for our district in Espanola Valley, deciding on Romero and his wicked curveball. I ended up playing centerfield and batting leadoff.

The game was a rare pitcher's duel as White Rock nipped us 1-0, despite an excellent effort from Joe Pat. He struck out 13 and allowed three hits. But the White Rock pitcher was just a tad better with his one-hit performance. My drag bunt became our only runner to reach base off of him.

As sad and frustrating as I think back on the setback, I at least made some kind of impact in the game. We went up against an imposing 6-foot pitcher, and at least I kept him from a night of perfection, laying the ball down and hustling to first base.

When I became bored, to pass the time I would pitch from my side of the property across the street to a nearby neighbor's wall. I even set up a strike zone painted in chalk. This is where I learned the strike zone. This is where I learned to paint a strike zone early on. I felt good about it, realizing I could do this all day long.

In a recent conversation with the granddaughter of a neighbor, she told me about the time her grandpa informed her about a kid on the next block who would be tirelessly throwing a rubber ball to the wall as he left for work in the morning. When he arrived back some eight hours later, the kid would still be throwing strikes.

Yes, that was me. I had a love for baseball, a **_Passion that lives in the core_**.

... One afternoon while my dad was at work, my teammate, pitcher and neighbor from 3BR & Construction, Cecil Chavez, came up with a neat idea. While my dad had what he thought was once the most beautiful, well-manicured Kentucky blue grass in the area, Cecil and I turned our thoughts to taking our pitching talents to the next level.

So we found a wheelbarrow, shovel and a pick that was stored in my dad's shed. Behind my house was a barren field that was often used as a baseball diamond. Unfortunately for me, it was a sore spot with my dad because it caused me several run-ins with the neighbors.

You see, I was always trying to see how far I could throw a baseball, but many times my throws would sail far into the sky and crack a window. I broke several, which put me in trouble with my dad for doing so.

In what took less than three hours, Cecil and I made what we thought was our 'Field of Dreams.' The mound was complete with pitching plate and a 12-inch downward slope to make it as authentic looking as a major league mound should look.

In the shed we came across an old unused steel mattress that had springs. We used a shoelace to make a square strike zone. When the ball was thrown in the strike zone, it shot back to the pitching mound.

It was great because you could now play by yourself if no one else was around.

ALONG CAME MAD DAD
Ages 11-12

Thinking of what I created, I forgot about dad, but not for long.

When he came home from work, I had hell to pay. He hissed and stood in total disbelief as I ruined his pride and joy. He quickly took what was once my short-lived 'Field of Dreams,' and made it into a cracked concrete in a deserted back yard.

But that memory was ever lasting. I ruined my dad's back yard in favor of a pitching mound that paved the way for my future success in the 'national pastime' of baseball.

Jack must have thought I was out of my mind even though he himself had taken a liking to baseball early on. When I was born, his playing days were cut short, but his own passion for the sport lived on. He would baby sit for me while my parents were at work. He probably figured that he could still be a part of the game while living vicariously through me.

Now, with a new pitching mound, being named an All-Star pitcher, Jack would spend all of his spare time in the back yard with me.

He was a perfectionist. He was demanding of his student. We would play catch for hours, then he would hit ground balls to me until he thought I'd had enough. On some days the practices were cut short due to my errant throws over the fence. Jack would not tolerate any bad throws. One too many and we went inside.

By being a disciplinarian, he instilled a lot of the key ingredients that took me to the next level.

At 12 years old, baseball had taken over in our household. By now Jack had passed on his passion for baseball card collecting to me. A few years earlier I had found a shoebox in our closet. In that shoebox were a thousand or so baseball cards dating back from 1957-61.

They were fabulous years to be a baseball card collector. In this stack, to name a few, were Willie Mays, Hank Aaron, Roger Maris, Yogi Berra, and Mickey Mantle. And the cards were in great condition.

I remember in my elementary years, Jack would sometimes pick me up after school. I especially enjoyed when it was payday for him. He would drive me to TG&Y and buy me several packs of baseball cards. My favorites were the 1975 set that included Nolan Ryan, George Brett and Pete Rose.

Ryan was my choice of pitchers. I would emulate his pitching motion from the left side with a high leg kick and a grunt as I let fly.

One of my last memories of elementary years was playing catch with my mom, Maude. As I recall, Jack and my dad were not around that day so I had to rely on my mom to catch me. We went into the front yard and I handed her the catcher's mitt. I was throwing about 80 percent that day so I wouldn't hurt her.

My mom was a trooper. She wanted the best for me. She could see that every time I played baseball, I had that twinkle in my eye. I might have been blessed with the hard work and dedication that I received from Jack and my dad, but it was actually my mom who provided me with the passion.

Mom allowed me to have fun. She thought it was ok for me to dream big. In my mind I was going to be a professional baseball pitcher and she often fueled my fire. It wasn't a matter of 'how', because I had the drive and determination. It was, indeed, a matter of 'when.'

After all, at this point in my life I had a fascination for baseball, and I had Jack in my back pocket.

As for Cecil Chavez, he later married, had a son named Kevin, and passed down his passion for baseball to him. Kevin Chavez was an All-State pitcher at St. Michael's, my alma mater, and was drafted in the 34th round by the Tampa Bay Rays. Arm injuries cut short Kevin's dreams of making it to the big leagues.

As I learned, in life we are sometimes associated with six degrees of separation.

LEARNING FROM THE BABE
Age 13

Anyway, by the time I reached junior high school, baseball remained one of the most important things in my life. Little League was now behind me, and the Babe Ruth League, with its new rules and baseball field dimensions, became the next challenge for me.

Although some of the names were familiar, I now had to compete against the best from Santa Fe. Some came from the Metropolitan LL, while others came from the American and National leagues. There were even some that played in high school, all of them between the ages of 13-15.

Yes, it was a different game alright.

You had 'flame throwers,' guys who could hit it out of the park due to the new field dimensions, and now as a pitcher, I had to hold runners on board. There were fast guys who could steal bases. So I had to make changes if I was to keep the dream alive.

The mound that Cecil Chavez and I had built in my backyard was now used only by Cecil when he came over. He was still only 11 years old and a Little League standout over at Metro.

And I had to figure out a way to get stronger so that I could compete with the other players.

My answer was right in my backyard, the same vacated field that was located behind my house, the same field where we gathered up enough dirt to build 'the mound.' It was the field that allowed my arm to become stronger.

Every day after school, I would rush home and meet Jack for a warm-up catch in my backyard. After we headed to the field, where on a daily basis, Jack would measure my long distance throws.

At one point, I heaved one 250 feet in the air, over a set of cactus plants that had always been a target of mine. Much to Jack's surprise, I had cleared the street and about another 70 feet of dirt that led to the cactus plants. Now Jack wasn't quick to get excited about anything, but he was impressed by the throw I uncorked that day.

The interesting thing about the long-toss sessions, added to the one-on-one pitching lessons and taking in the mechanics told by Jack, was keeping in shape, the same shape that would mold a career that would take me to multiple countries around the world without ever having to go through a surgery or a major arm injury for over 44 years.

How could Jack know all this? It was simple in fact. Play, support and live vicariously with a younger brother, who had the passion and the love for the game of baseball. He must have seen something that was invisible to me at a young age.

Baseball kept him young at heart.

Baseball gave me a reason to dream at night. And think at other times.

So getting back to that giant toss thrown in the backyard, I now set my sights on the deserted ditch that lay beyond the cactus plants. If I could get my body to heave a throw in that area, I was looking at 300 plus feet. I now had something to aim at.

And of course there was the challenge of St. Michael's, which I entered as a 7th grader.

I was befriended by two likeable baseball cousins: Ron Noedel and Paul Romero. They were baseball fanatics as well, and were Little League All-Stars in their respective American and National leagues. We were always getting harassed by the baseball upperclassmen in the hallways, as we wore to school every day our LL All-Star jackets with matching cap.

We all got along great and managed a friendship, with baseball as our number one bond together. We ate, drank and slept baseball. And for lunch break, we would bring our gloves to school and play catch on the varsity baseball field, hoping to one day be on the team.

We were all dreamers.

My first year in Babe Ruth was kind of a wash. Although I did get experience playing with high school guys, some of whom were destined to play in other sports when at the college level. You could just see the talent they displayed.

One became the quarterback of a state high school champion and went on to star in college at the West Point Academy. Another was a gifted athlete in both baseball and basketball. He started on the basketball court as a freshman at New Mexico State.

These two players provided a great deal of leadership for me in my rookie year. I watched, listened and learned as much as I could from these two. It was another reason that I thought it was great being a part of the Capital Ford baseball team that summer of 1977.

Going off with my dad on a trip to visit both my brothers now living in the Midwest probably cost me a chance of being voted on to the 13-year-old All-Star team.

Not even my own coach gave me a vote. I was upset. I felt now that I had something to prove.

HURLING FOR THE HORSEMEN
Ages 16-17

First, I had something to prove in high school. At St. Michael's, nothing came easy for me. I had to work hard to achieve an average grade. Between the classroom and the baseball field, I had to put in twice the work.

Coming into my sophomore year following what I described as a "breakout" summer in the Babe Ruth League, I was now focusing all of my energy to get a chance to show what I could do on the mound. All I dreamed about was getting a chance to pitch in high school.

By now, Jack was pretty much out of the picture as a practice force. He was now a mentor, fan, my numero uno critic. He was now a force on the 'outside'. He would not miss any of my games for the next 30 years. He became my shadow in baseball. I was his protégé, his life-long project in the making.

And so I wanted to take the hill and pass on what I had been taught. I was now a sophomore in the spring of 1980 when Horsemen head baseball coach Richard Alarid had probably noticed some positive things in practice and figured I deserved a chance.

My control was better than average. My heat was just warming up. While Alarid felt that he had an "Ace in the making," he thought he would find out quickly by starting me against 4A Los Alamos HS in a non-district game.

I was ready for the moment. So was assistant coach Bob Chavez. He had watched me pitch numerous times in my Little League and Babe Ruth days. He had coached me and had plenty of confidence in me.

Fortunately for me, the game was to be played at home, so I had my family, schoolmates and the familiar field on my side. My mother was sitting there in her white Cadillac, honking the horn after every one of my strikeouts. Jack, my dad, sister and nephew were also in the stands.

In my mind, it was definitely an historic event at our household as I put the Hilltoppers down in a five-hit, complete-game triumph. The headlines in the local newspaper the next day read "Gem of Consistency" for the Horsemen.

And I was on cloud nine. I was a winning pitcher on my varsity team. My family was so proud they presented me with the game ball. They also started a fad of collecting game-winning balls, which continued on up to the present.

By now my family finally realized that I was a pretty good baseball player. They now pieced together the puzzling times that Jack spent on preparing me for these times. As for Jack, he figured that the sky was the limit.

Meanwhile, Alarid basked in the limelight for a week. He looked good starting me against Los Alamos. Now he figured he'd bring me down to earth by starting me against Santa Fe High School, our biggest rivals, our Siringo Road neighbors. The Demons, though, had players that were on another level. Many of the city's finest players donned their roster.

Rod Tafoya and James Trujillo

After but three innings, I was pulled. SFHS had turned us back to the tune of 13-1. Even though the loss was catastrophic, it was just the experience I needed in my young pitching career.

As the season went on, I was delegated to the bullpen. There, my confidence increased and I learned more about how to pitch.

When the regular season was over, I and some of my teammates tried out for the Post 101 American Legion team. Loaded with Demon players who hit me and the rest of our hurlers, this was a talent-laden squad.

With added knowledge now, I was now looking toward the Mickey Owen Baseball Camp in Miller, Mo, and was joined by my closest friends, Ron Noedel and Paul Romero. First I had to convince my parents that it was the right thing to do. I told them that, with my eye on college, I needed all the assistance I could get. Jack was in my corner and my parents gave the okay.

Next stop, Miller, Mo, except the airlines were at a standstill. If we wanted to go, we'd have to find another way to travel. Enter the Greyhound Bus.

Twenty five hours later, the bus dropped us off in the Ozarks. It was different temperature that's for sure. For two weeks, it was hot and muggy. Even the campers were different, some with twangs from the south, others with eastern accents. They all had a field day with us.

They asked things like, "Do you all eat beans and rice down there in Mexico,"?

At the camp, I was inspired by one of the head instructors, a cocky, short, left-handed former Major League pitcher by the name of Jerry Nyman. He pitched for the Chicago White Sox in the late 60s and for the San Diego Padres in 1970.

He talked about striking out the Oakland A's Reggie Jackson several times. He told about pitching for Brigham Young University before signing as a free agent with the White Sox at age 22. He spoke of winning 16 games at minor league Sarasota in Florida before climbing up to the big leagues for three seasons.

He was small in stature at 5-10 and weighed only 165 pounds. He provided me with inspiration. I was in awe that he made the big leagues being as small and as wily as he was.

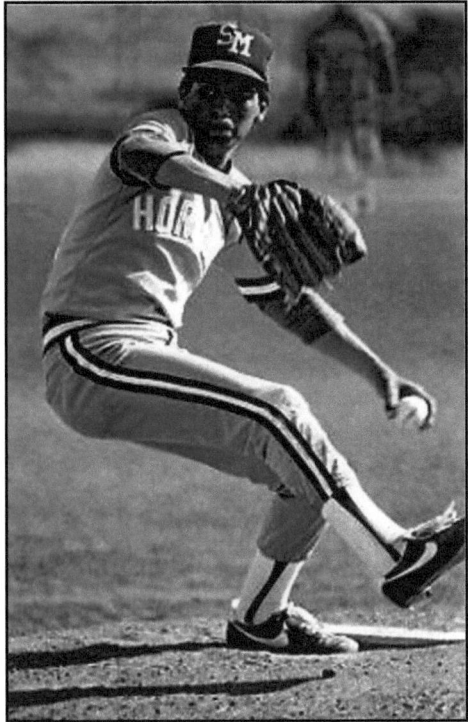

RIOS, ROMERO, MY RIVALS ON THE HILL
Ages 16-17

The experience of the camp was a wonderful thing for myself, Ron and Paul. When we returned to Santa Fe, we were eager to move on to the American Legion level. From that point on, we were mainstays as rookies, with those two weeks of professional instruction under our belts.

It was Nyman who taught me to throw a slider. It was about a decade later, that while pitching professionally in the New York-Pennsylvania League, that while looking at the roster of the Welland Pirates, that I recognized a familiar name in the program.

Jerry Nyman, pitching coach, it said. And so I walked up to him before the game and told him that I had met him at the Mickey Owen Baseball Camp in 1980. Not only did he remember me, but he still walked and talked with a definite swagger.

With St. Michael's, it wasn't about walking and talking with a definite swagger. I hadn't reached that stage yet. Now, it was competition against fierce high school rivals.

One in particular was Victor Rios of Pojoaque High. He was a pitching star, my nemesis, my rival, and my fiercest competitor on the diamond. In one year alone we faced each other three times, with Rios coming away with 1-0 and 4-3 wins. I did put together a 2-1 victory at home with 16 strikeouts and allowing only three hits.

I even scored both of our runs, the deciding one coming when the Elks' catcher tried desperately to take me out at home as I slid in safely.

They were masterful pitching duals between us. We battled with ferocity and became such rivals that we never spoke to each other throughout our high school years. Pitching against Pojoaque was like pitching against the enemy. But it was those match-ups that put me on the map.

For my efforts and hard work, an All-District Team selection was in the making, as both an outfielder and as a starting pitcher. I was happy with the way I swung the bat.

I was happy to wear my St. Michael's uniform. It included a blue jacket that read Horsemen across the letters and an adjustable blue cap that said St. M in red and white.

When we were eliminated in the playoffs in May of 1979, I began my final season as a Babe Ruth player. I was now going to be counted on heavily as the ace of the Capital Ford pitching staff.

But with success comes defeat, close ones that remain with you.

And so I was penciled in later that summer to pitch against my former Metro League rival, Joe Pat Romero. For the first time in over three years, we were facing each other as experienced aces of the league.

It was a reunion of Metro All-Stars.

I thought of it as being an epic pitching matchup, us against Joe Pat and the Colony Builders. I was correct.

We matched zeros for the first five innings before Colony scored once for a 1-0 lead. After seven innings, the duel resulted in a tough defeat for me, but Joe Pat had it all that time. He didn't allow a hit, struck out 18, and displayed his curveball wizardry.

I wasn't that bad. I was reached for only three hits and mowed down 15 on strikes.

Some 20 years later, I actually presented Joe Pat with the same game ball for his trophy case. Until then, I had kept the game ball as usual, and, as was my habit, I had the game's statistics on it, *his* stats.

That summer, something odd happened. My left arm had grown to another level, a new level that even Jack had no answer for. As he was a big proponent of control, my fastball was now a left-handed moving blazer that was always tailing. When we played catch together, I had to be careful not to frustrate Jack.

He was still my greatest asset and both a mentor and motivator.

We moved from the back yard, which could no longer "hold" my game. We usually went to my Babe Ruth League field, which was now called Fort Marcy. It was perfect for what we needed.

On one particular summer day, we jumped the back fence and headed to the field where it had all started for one last long toss.

I went to my usual spot and spotted Jack in the ditch before the 'record throw' in the cactus plants.

I recall throwing over 10 tosses that day and hit the back of the ditch for what amounted to a heave of over 300 feet. My arm was feeling great and becoming stronger, and, much to Jack's amazement, I was on course to becoming a 'full time' pitcher.

At the end of the season, my last one, I was selected to the Babe Ruth All-Star team. I was one of the old experienced veterans on the squad, and was being counted on for both pitching and outfield duties.

The majority of the team was split up of varsity and junior varsity players from rivals St. Michael's and Santa Fe High.

We played the state tournament in Artesia. We knocked off Portales in the opener and then surprised a talented team from Albuquerque behind Joe Pat's curveballs. We next fell to Belen, 3-2, which eventually won the tournament, in extra innings.

I played centerfield. I made several outstanding throws home and nailed a couple of runners from scoring. I batted .636. I made the all-tournament team.

Even though I wasn't on the mound each game, Jack and I both felt that my 'arm' was now getting the attention and I was getting the respect I had worked for.

FRESHMAN YEAR
A TIME TO LEARN
Age 15

My freshman year at St. Michael's did not begin as I had hoped for. In fact, I was initially disappointed. After several of my fellow ninth-graders made the varsity, I was not one of them.

The pressure was intense.

One day as I was heading to the field, I was summoned by coach Alarid to the dugout.

"Hey, I'm going to have to cut you," he says. "We're going with a young team and I already have seven freshmen here."

He topped it off with a backhand across my chest. This was something he did to you if he liked you. But I stood there in total amazement, total disbelief. There weren't any words exchanged.

I'm thinking, what was Jack going to think? In my mind, I was going to be the laughing stock of the school. Making the team as a freshman meant everything to me. And Jack.

As I sulked to the locker room with my head hanging in anger, I sat in front of my locker and began to change out of my baseball uniform. I did not want to go home and face the embarrassment from the family. After all, my brother Glenn was a Horseman varsity letterman. I felt that I had let them all down, especially myself.

As I was slipping into my slacks, I was interrupted by fellow freshman, Kenny Pacheco, who came in hollering, "Rod, Rod, coach Alarid wants to see you. Come quick."

I thought to myself that maybe coach wants me to be the scorekeeper or even the water boy. This bothered me.

But when I walked on to the baseball field, Alarid looked at me with those blue eyes, chewing bubble gum as he grinned with his head tilted to the side as he laid yet another hand to my chest.

"Come here, Tafoya, come here," he says. "Listen here, I made a mistake. You can surely help us out. You're back on. Here's your jacket and cap."

I still get choked up when I remember this turn of events. I got a second chance. Now I could go home and tell my family that I made the St. Michael's varsity. I was there with Ron, Paul and five other freshmen. It was to that point the happiest day of my life.

On a sad note, Kenny was cut and was the odd man out. I had buried that moment in the back of my head for 31 years without saying a word about it. It was my first taste of perseverance.

Also remembered was that I never took the mound that freshmen season. I platooned with Paul in right field. But Paul started in right as we entered the 3A playoffs against favored Artesia. We were eliminated.

But in my last two years in high school, my passion for baseball grew to a new level, with my fastball being clocked at 82-85 miles an hour. With the control that I had, my work ethic, and discipline, it was the edge I needed to compete with the state's best athletes.

MY ARM WAS NOW GOING TO COLLEGE
Age 19

Everything else was behind me. Little League, Babe Ruth League, Mickey Owen Baseball Camp, St. Michael's.

Ahead was college, an entire new experience, another challenge, but on a higher level. I had learned that then-NAIA New Mexico Highlands in Las Vegas, N.M., was interested in me.

At the same time, I was always dreaming of leaving the state and playing for a baseball program on my 'dream' list. NMHU was not one of them.

But the school – about an hour's drive down I-25 – had the best offer for me. It was planning on a rebuilding year and needed help on the mound. Aside from the full-ride offer, there was a great opportunity to pitch immediately, to make an impact as a freshman, and a chance to be close enough for mom's home cooking.

Bob Chavez was head coach of the Horsemen my senior year. I had had previous conversations with him, but none regarding talks about playing at the college level.

Now I had to face reality. A new wave of baseball players were heading to college. Of my St. Michael's teammates, Steve Arias signed with junior college national power Yavapai Roughriders, Ron Noedel with St. Mary's of the Plains in Dodge City, Kan., and James Trujillo, our catcher, was focused on Glendale in Arizona.

And my pitching rival and nemesis, Victor Rios, was headed to Western Arizona Community College, a school that was high on my list.

But again, NMHU served up the best offer.

Even Jack took part in the process. He was now a part-time agent, college advisor, and admissions counselor. His immediate thought was that I'd be crazy not to accept this offer. He was so helpful with the process, even assisting me with Grant paperwork to finish the course of action.

He even went out of his way to suggest that I choose business management as my college major. That was the scary part. I just didn't feel that I was smart enough to handle the load. But Jack assured me that he'd assist me if I required help.

Brothers Jack, Glenn and Jim all had their degrees and it was time for little brother to get his via the free way. Even my dad had to let out a sigh of relief, and he had Jack to be thankful for, especially for the big-time money that he saved my parents for the price tag of a college education.

But what my dad never understood was that I could get a college degree and play baseball at the same time. The only part of the deal was that while there, I always had to pass a minimum of 12 credit hours, while managing to play the best baseball that I could accomplish.

For me, the trade-off was simple. Go to school and get a passing grade and you get to play baseball another day. I had great respect for the game. It meant everything to me. Being the first in my family to attend college and to play baseball was a privilege to me, and I was going to do anything and everything I could to be successful.

And so my next stop was New Mexico Highlands. And as practice began that fall, there were three other freshmen players from Santa Fe that were also on scholarship and trying to make the final roster. They were Santa Fe HS graduates Paul Baca, Jamie Graham and Eddie Padilla.

After an intense four months of practice, we took the road to Lubbock Christian College in Texas, and then to the University of El Paso (UTEP). Fortunately, Paul and I made the traveling squad, Paul as an outfielder, and myself as the designated long reliever on the mound.

We were a young team and not on the same level as our competition. Heading back to Las Vegas, we were 0-8. By mid-March, it was evident that we were headed for one of the worst seasons in the school's history on the diamond. At this point, we stood at 4-

18, with a team ERA of 9.88, and our offense was sparse at 4.58 runs per game.

But I was gaining experience by pitching mop-up innings. With this, head coach Jim Abreu gave me my first start following my impressive outing in a 10-7 comeback over Denver University.

Trailing 7-1 in the fifth inning with no out, I was summoned from the bullpen and managed to strike out five Pioneers while giving up only three hits, and keeping them scoreless allowed us to rally for the exciting victory.

Now it was time for my first start. My opponent would be no easy task in Trinidad, a junior college powerhouse known for winning and getting players drafted to the professional level. I was looking at a Trinidad team with a 29-7 record and mucho offensive power.

Well, I showed a lively fastball as my family watched from the stands. After a 10-strikeout effort, I lost a 7-6 squeaker. I was now a freshman on a 5-21 team who was getting his feet wet with relatively no pressure. Heck, I even kept the game ball.

In mid-April, I was given another relief stint. Playing Lamar JC at home, I was brought in with the score 8-8 after five innings. I threw two innings of shutout ball, struck out two, and we scored once in the seventh for a 9-8 victory.

I had added confidence as the Rocky Mountain Athletic Conference tournament approached.

N. M. H. U. BASEBALL TEAM

Team members are: Botton Row - Left to Right: Scott Bradbury, Barry Jimenez, Carlos Hernandez, Kelly Carpenter, Joe Garcia, Rodney Tafoya, and Jeff Austin. 2nd Row - Left to Right: Jeff Kittler, Bill Howard, Louie Zubia, Armando Chaires, Dwayne Martinez, and Larry Garcia. 3rd Row - Left to Right: Joe Pacheco, David Gonzales, Aaron Cajero, Terry Tiner, and Joe Cazares. 4th Row - Left to Right: Leo Escapita, Ralph Porter, Jeff Trujillo, Jamie Graham, and Robert Giddings. 5th Row Left to Right: Asst. Coach Rick Wright, Mike Trujillo, Rich Gutierrez, Kevin Ratcliff, Bobby Garcia, and Brad Ficklin, and Head Coach Jim Marshall. Last Row - Left to Right: Trainer-George Tonkin and Asst. Coach-Arnold Stapleton.

TIME FOR BEISBOL IN MEXICO
Age 20

With the RMAC tournament now upon us, coach Abreu decided to do the unthinkable, as in start a freshman in game one against second-seeded Mesa State.

His thought was to ride the positive relief appearances that I had made, that I had given the team a chance to rest our starting staff, and finish out games two and three of the double elimination tourney.

And so I took the mound in place of junior right-handed starter Jose (Pepe) Alvarado, who I had come in for when we trailed 7-1 against Denver University, and when I held the Pioneers scoreless while we rallied to win.

Alvarado was born in Mexico, in Juarez, Chihuahua, and went on to attend Hatch High School. He was a large man, standing over 6-3, and often traveled down south to pitch in Mexico. Being an overly nice guy that he was, there wasn't any animosity towards me, as he felt it was in the best interests of the team.

He agreed that I was the hottest hurler on the Cowboys, and, like all of us, just wanted to win.

My opponent that day was Darryl Akerfelds, a transfer from the University of Arkansas, who later pitched in the big leagues and worked as a pitching coach for the Major League Oakland Athletics.

Facing an opposing 6-5 pitcher, I was unfazed and looked forward to the opportunity to compete.

All of my teammates patted me on the back, including team captain and leading hitter Gary Tripp. They were all in agreement with Abreu that I should start the game. This was my biggest opportunity thus far. It was on a stage I knew nothing about.

I was going to throw my best game possible.

But the end result was both teams pounding away for nine innings, and it became a disappointing 9-7 setback, a no-decision for me, and we were then eliminated from the tournament.

On the other hand, I came away unscathed with more experience than the day before. What was now going to be what I thought to be a restful summer, I thought wrong. It became the turning point of a much well-traveled baseball career with priceless opportunities.

For, as finals began my freshmen year, Alvarado had summoned me to his apartment. He and his soon-to-be-wife, Julie, had an opportunity for me.

Pepe, is what he was called, would be pitching in Juarez for Muebles Zeta, a furniture company that had its own semi-pro team. Complete with payroll, they paid their players a salary that included meals (a steak and a bottle of beer after games), gas money, and a hotel when needed.

Alvarado had it all figured out. He had the use of his sister's house in Las Cruces, NM, and it was about an hour's drive to Juarez. He was set to be a part-time lifeguard for the summer and all he needed was a mound partner and roommate.

It was an offer that I couldn't pass up, and all I needed was assurance from my parents and a lift from Jack, my new acting advisor.

All Pepe needed from me was an answer.

It was late May and I felt it was a chance to embark on a new journey, a solo journey for the first time in my life. My arm and I were taking a journey to manhood through the game of baseball.

Except this wouldn't be ordinary baseball, it was baseball along the Mexican border, and they called it "Beisbol."

One thing that I had with my family was trust. They knew they had given me the tools to survive, and now that I was a college kid, it brought me more bargaining power. On the other hand, no crazy parents were going to allow their kid to go to some foreign land and play baseball, but mine did. They knew the main reason I went to college was to play baseball and earn a college degree. They were synonymous. I couldn't do one without the other.

This was my plan of attack.

I used baseball to get away that summer with such conviction, my family had no choice but to let me have my way. With no money saved up, my family felt that my happiness wavered on my success in college.

And after all the questions and answers had gone back and forth, my parents gave me the okay. I could now drive to Las Cruces in my new Monte Carlo that my parents had purchased for me. I was, to say the least, a trend-setter.

With a pocket full of cash to pay a few months' rent, I headed to meet Pepe. He had arranged a tryout for me in Juarez that weekend, as the brass from Muebles Zeta were out in droves to see the new American import, me.

I found out very quickly that both the language barrier and driving in Mexico were frightening combinations. I now had to put all of my trust in Alvarado, for he was the closest thing to family in these times.

With over nine months of straight pitching, my arm was in terrific shape and I easily made the team. Pepe and I were the aces of the staff, and it was great having a lefty and a righty in the rotation.

SURDO RENE
&
THE LANGUAGE BARRIER
Age 19

Now Alvarado, being from Juarez, spoke fluent Spanish. As for myself, not learning the language when I was young hindered me, and I paid the price in my first game there.

The players were very eager to meet the foreigner or "extranjero" as we were called. And Pepe decided that I would have a different given name for the time that I pitched in the state of Chihuahua.

As none of the players could properly pronounce "Rod" or "Rodney", Pepe had some fun with me and proclaimed my name be "Rene"

For the summer, I was known as Surdo (lefty) and Rene.

But, on the other hand, I was not very fond of my new namesake, and making headlines in the Mexican newspapers as "Rene" didn't make a hit with me.

But I quickly got over it, as I was making headlines on the mound as a young "Surdo", a much followed commodity in Mexico.

My debut in Juarez fell on Mother's Day, and fittingly, I pitched a complete game with 14 strikeouts against the Airport Auxiliary Team. During the first month, I gained added experience and finished with a 2-0 record and 1.71 ERA in 26 innings with 31 strikeouts.

Both Alvarado and I were selected for a regional team that was chosen from the best players from the North Division. In one start and one relief appearance, I went 1-0, struck out an even dozen, and compiled a 1.29 ERA.

Things were definitely going my way as my arm was getting the work it craved in the warm weather. As our team finished third, I now headed home in mid-June, thinking I had had enough of the border town of Juarez.

Back in Santa Fe, my date and I decided to take I-25 to watch the Albuquerque Dukes of the AAA Pacific Coast League on a Friday night. With my fresh accomplishments in the back of my mind, I was summoned to the press box area by the surprising announcement of, "Paging Rod Tafoya, please report to the press box area."

Expecting the worst, I informed my date that I would return momentarily. On the telephone was my mom, informing me that the president of the Juarez club had called and invited me to pitch for the upcoming "Chihuahua Estatal", or state all-star team known as the Indios de Juarez.

If that wasn't enough, my family sent friend, Nestor Romero, with two months of packed luggage to find me and drive me to the airport as the brass from Juarez had a round-trip airline ticket from Albuquerque to Juarez. From there, Romero drove my date back to Santa Fe.

It was my mom who came away as the champion that she is, bluntly letting the Juarez president know that they won't get their "surdo" unless they paid my expenses. My mom certainly knew how to wheel and deal. She made it clear that getting my servicing wasn't going to be cheap.

Once in the border city, I took a taxi cab to meet the team. Pepe was there to greet me. My next step was walking onto the chartered bus that would take us to the field of play.

"Congratulations! You've been selected to represent the entire Zone One that will compete for the state title in Chihuahua." That was the banner displayed on the bus.

That was nice to see, and the trip would also take in scenic sites I never imagined. My travels would now take me to new places like Jimenez, Delicias, Cuauhtemoc, Parral, Casas Grandes, and Chihuahua.

I felt like a professional and was getting wined and dined for the services of my arm, my left one of course.

Little did I know that the NAIA would prohibit such behavior. I was too naïve to know better. I was just proud to be pitching in a foreign land and best of all, winning.

As our Juarez team finished fourth in the Chihuahua state playoffs, I was basking with an entire new appreciation for baseball. With more hard work on my horizon, I was beginning to envision a future in the sport.

I had just proven that I could pitch to a different level. I was 5-0, struck out 71 batters in 65 innings, and turned in a stingy 1.78 ERA in a foreign land.

Photograph by Nick Sedillos

THE ARM LIVES
SOUTH OF THE BORDER
Age 20

Back on campus, Alvarado and I kept to ourselves so we wouldn't be expelled from the NAIA for accepting what we did. Airline tickets, meals, hotels, and cash under the table were reasons to strike out our college eligibility. Of course, in our minds, we merely did it for the love of the game.

So it was now my sophomore season at NMHU, and Pepe and I had enough baseball stories and experiences to last a lifetime. Looking back on this, our naivety got caught up in all the hype. We wanted to compete and continue playing baseball even if it meant taking my arm to another country.

I didn't seem to mind. I knew I was well liked in Mexico. I knew I could have a future there if it came to that. At the same time, I thought up what I thought was a great idea. I decided to write every major league organization and tell them of a "lefty" who was pitching for the NMHU Cowboys and perhaps deserved a look.

By Christmas time of that year, the letters started rolling in.

From the Detroit Tigers, I opened up one signed by their general manager Roger Jongewaard.

From the San Francisco Giants, there was one from a scout named Gene Thompson, who said he'd plan a trip to see me pitch in the early spring.

Then there was the Kansas City Royals, whose GM responded by saying he would come to watch me.

In all, I received 27 letters. I thought it was a great Christmas present. I was now getting a feeling that baseball was in my distant future. Whether it was the states or Mexico, I was going to follow my dream.

As my college season ended and more experience came my way, including a win over Division One New Mexico State, I was ready to return to Mexico for my second year there.

Alvarado had now graduated and was hoping to sign a professional contract in the AAA Liga Mexicana (Mexican League), where legendary players like Satchel Paige, Warren Spahn and Josh Gibson headed south for a taste of Latin baseball.

As for myself, I was now a sophomore and was not eligible for the Major League draft until my junior year. So I put that topic in the back burner and focused on getting better and getting my arm stronger.

My only setback was my size, or lack of. Baseball officials salivated on tall pitchers with 90 mph fastballs. I had neither, so I figured I was better off hurling in Mexico knowing I had a chance there. Down there, they just wanted outs. They didn't care how tall you were. Plus most pitchers had screwballs and an assortment of stuff I had never heard of before.

As school ended in May, my sister's friend in El Paso, Tex., was seeking to rent her house for the summer. It was a perfect solution for me as I headed to pitch for Muebles Zeta in Juarez.

With a new car, a bachelor pad, and my new paper route, I was ready for round two in Juarez.

Alvarado and I picked up where we left off the previous campaign. By our second start, a Mexican scout by the name of Seibu met us during our customary beer and steak postgame celebration on the grounds of Muebles Zeta, which now had its own private stadium built on site.

As always, Pepe was our translator, and I could tell by the way he was intently listening and smiling that it was something good.

We were then whisked away to Cruz Blanca Stadium where the AAA Mexico City Tigres (Tigers) were in town for a four-game series against the home town Indios de Juarez. Most important, it was a true tryout and a chance to get signed by a pro team.

It was such a big deal that my brother Glenn and mom drove down from Santa Fe to support me in my initial pro tryout.

But immediately upon seeing the frame and fastball of the 6-3, 205-pound Alvarado, the Tigres quickly signed him to a noteworthy contract on the spot as their fifth starter.

Being a 19-year-old wily left-hander, the Tigres had other plans for me. They wanted to sign me but were inclined to send me to their farm team – the AA Liga Norte de Sonora of the Sonora League located in Caborca, Chihuahua.

It sounded wonderful to me, but not to my mom. She informed the Tigres' brass that the talk would go no further, that to call her at home to discuss future plans after I finished my college education.

That done, I headed back to pitch for Muebles Zeta the following week. I also had an empty feeling in my stomach, as Pepe was no longer around and the loneliness that surrounded me grew worse as I wondered where I'd be next.

To add to the mix, I had worked my tail off as a newspaper boy, waking up at 3 each morning and failing to understand that I was to pay myself from all the checks and cash that I had collected over a month's time on the job. So my boss said he told me what to do, and because I didn't, I wouldn't receive any pay.

Now I had no money and there was plenty of uncertainty surrounding my baseball career.

So now my mom was in contact with the Tigres with the hope that they would assign me to the AAA Mexican League's developmental training camp.

It worked. I was now ready to leave the state of Chihuahua and head deep into Southern Mexico where the AAA Mexican League players were made.

HISS IN THE MITT IN PASTEJE
Age 20

El gringo was heading south again. This time, it was to a place so remote, you couldn't even locate it on a map. All I knew was that it was outside of Mexico City, somewhere in between Atlacomulco and Toluca, and that they label it the Districto Federal (Federal District).

There, I was met by the Tigres' brass, who had struck a deal with my mom to play in what was called Academia Pasteje.

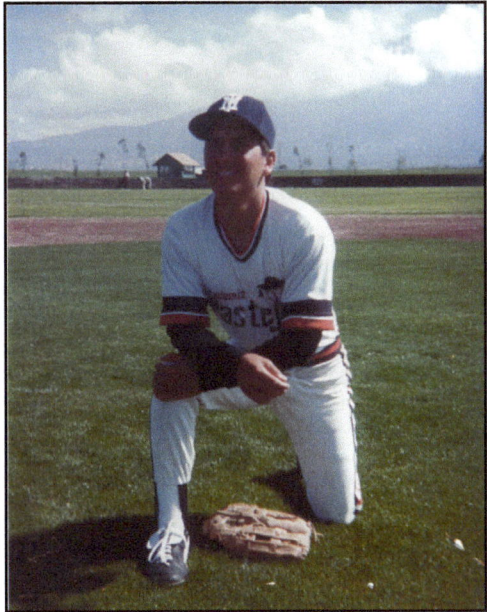

This was the brainwork of the team's assistant coach, Ozzie Alvarez, who with the backing of the AAA Mexican League opened an invitation-only baseball academy that produced the best young crop of talent in all of Mexico.

The top 100 prospects from the country were invited, then sent to a remote farm that produced a yearly draft of baseball talent that even the major leagues would try and hand-pick if they were good enough prospects.

Top baseball scouts, including Mike Brito, who signed pitcher Fernando Valenzuela, were frequent visitors.

Many of these players were legendary stars of the Mexican League, some of them even making it to the 'big show.'

One of these players was a tall side-armed fast-baller named Isidro Marquez. He played in the Dodgers' organization, moving up to AA San Antonio before heading back to the AAA Mexican League. He made his mark in the mid-90s upon receiving a promotion to pitch in the big leagues for the White Sox.

At nearly 40, his main claim to fame was in 2004, when he pitched Mexico past the USA Olympic Team, 2-1, and his country qualified for the Greece Olympics. It was the only time in history that a United States baseball team failed to make it to the Olympic Games.

When I first knew him, Marquez was a tall, lean, quiet kid. Only 18 years old and full of funny antics, he pulled one of the worst pranks on me. He caught a snake and put it in the webbing of my glove. I hated snakes, always did, still do.

As I reached for my glove and placed my right hand in the mitt, I heard a hiss. I jumped and screamed much to the delight of Marquez and the rest of the young prospects. They all giggled in amazement. They loved playing tricks on the 'extranjero'.

While in college in Wichita, Kan., some years later, I saw Marquez pitching for the AA San Antonio Missions and made certain to remind him of the snake incident. He laughed at me for quite a while.

I was the first American to attend Pasteje, as it was a place for passionate baseball players who aspired to make it to the Mexican League, which was the country's version of big league ball.

It gave prospects a chance to see the world through baseball without getting an education. They came from all walks of life, from places like Puerto Vallarta, Mazatlan, Acapulco ... They all came with the passion to someday make it in the popular sport.

With some luck, when the scouts came for the Mexican League's annual baseball draft, players would be chosen, offered a contract, and live the baseball dream. The others would receive a paid bus ticket to return to where they came from.

This meant they would have to start all over again and choose a different path other than baseball. Also, life in Mexico was tough. Work an 8-hour day and claim a few dollars for your efforts.

I always felt bad for my teammates that never made it. I often wondered what became of them and where they ended up. For the fortunate ones, they were able to live the rock-star lifestyle. They would have progressive clothes to wear, stay at lavish hotels, and receive daily meal money, as well as traveling and being part of a team.

Baseball offered them everything that real-life Mexico couldn't promise.

Back on the farm, it was hard work. I learned that playing with Mexico's best prospects was my way out of the states if I didn't make it there. The only difference with me and these guys was that I was going to get a college degree and not have to pay for it when it was done.

I relied on my southpaw arm all these years, from Little League through high school, and now I was rubbing shoulders with the best that Mexico had to offer. I was finding out at a young age that travel and baseball were fueling my fire and desire to compete. Pasteje offered everything to the imagination baseball-wise.

You ate, slept and drank baseball 10 to 12 hours a day. Wake up call was at five in the morning. Then we ran for an hour, lifted weights for an hour, and then ate breakfast. At eight o'clock, buses were lined up waiting to take all the players to the baseball fields.

At nine o'clock, the fun began.

Batters would practice hitting drills while others swung fiercely to a stationary tire, where often their hands bled from prolonged periods of swinging. Other times, they made us crawl under wires, reminding me of the basic drills required in the military.

It was simply utter torture at Pasteje.

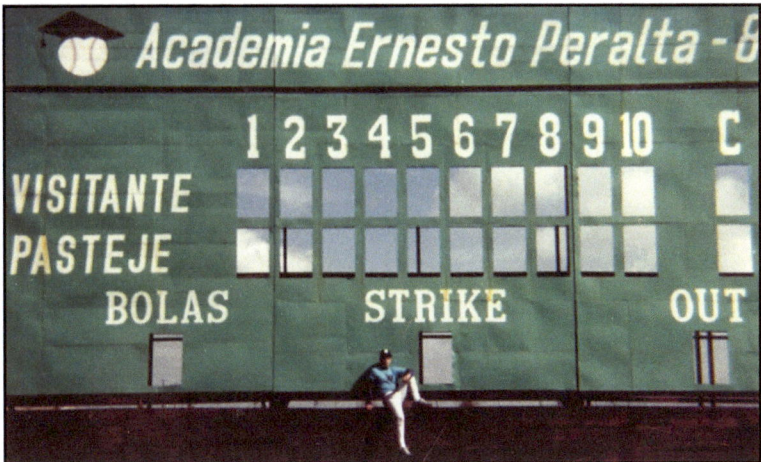

TIME FOR TRAVELING MUSIC
Age 20

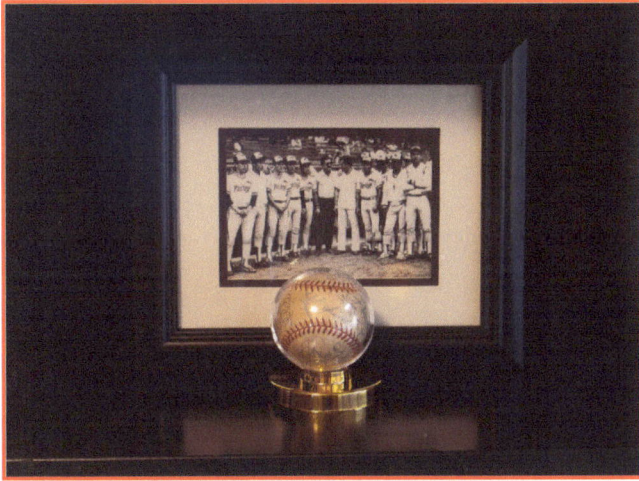

Photograph by Nick Sedillos

With all these up in the morning out on the job work to do as baseball campers, we had no problem hitting the sack when day was done.

But in the wee small hours of the morning, we were up again, doing what we were here to do. Pitchers worked on drills over and over again until the drills were mastered. Although there were plenty of instructions tossed around, we only wanted to play.

And while the scrimmages were good, I always dreamed of the live games.

On Sundays, the camp would send its best to the DF to partake in a game played at the AAA Tigres

Stadium (Parque Seguro Social), in which crowds of 30,000 beisbol-crazy fans had a ball.

In my lone start there, I was victorious as the legendary Mexican Hall of Famer, Hector Espino, the country's version of Babe Ruth, watched from the top step of the dugout.

After the game, I was fortunate to receive a photograph and autographed baseball from Espino, who posed with me and Detroit Tiger third baseman Aurelio Rodriguez.

That was neat. Otherwise, as I said, it was utter torture at Pasteje. If you weren't obsessed with baseball, you didn't belong there. But I felt I did, for from that point on in my life I knew I had adoration for the game.

And deep down, I felt that no one could go through that experience and not love the game. It was endless baseball. It was heaven.

Within the barracks, though, it wasn't heaven, At best, it was interesting to say the least. No phone calls, no visitation, no leaving the premises.

To get a decent snack, you had to break out in the middle of the night, as a group of us did. We had flash lights and found an endless trail to nowhere. Once, we found a shack and knocked until we woke up the owners of the small storefront.

With the money stipend that the academy gave us, we brought back all we could carry.

Luckily for me, I still had college to finish and two more years of eligibility left in my arm. My travels to Mexico thus far were something to write about. Funny thing was, I'd be back!

But first there was my junior year at New Mexico Highlands. It was to be an odd, yet different season. I had just lost my roommate and best friend, Paul Baca, when he decided to transfer to New Mexico State to be with his girlfriend.

To make matters worse, coach Abreu was out as head coach and was replaced by Jim Marshall, who had an entirely different approach to baseball and things in general.

Marshall was not new to the Cowboy program as he led the '67 team to its only NAIA national title. He may have been legendary, but the program was again in a rebuilding phase and I was getting tired of the baseball politics that were going on.

I was a junior and veteran on the mound. I had no time to fool around with my future, so I pondered a change. I started looking elsewhere.

I used coach Marshall to push me out of the program without him even realizing it. I had returned from Mexico with even more confidence. I now thought I could compete with just about anyone or so I believed.

My interest was now in the Jayhawk League. I had heard about it from some of our conference's best players. Scouts loved it because it was a hotbed for experienced college players and would-be professional prospects. It joined the Alaskan League and Cape Cod League as the top three college leagues at the time.

I immediately let it be known to coach Marshall that I wanted a crack at the Jayhawk League. I explained that it would be a way to develop my chances to pitch professionally if I was ever going to make my dream come true.

By the end of the NMHU season, I packed my bags and, along with Larry Garcia, my heavy-hitting teammate, we drove in my car to Wichita, Kan., in hopes of making the Wichita Broncos' baseball team.

The team had recently relocated from Hutchinson, Kan., where the likes of Barry Bonds, Pete Incaviglia, Odibee McDowell, Will Clark, Rafael Palermo, and Mike Brantley all played the previous season.

There were, however, some tough shoes to fill. The team was built around the genius baseball mind of Dick King, who took pride in recruiting the nation's finest college talent.

As the first players to arrive, King quickly made us feel right at home. My pitching coach was Paul Sanagorski, once a successful coach from Newman College, which was now Division 2 Newman University.

We hit it off immediately. He was the first coach to teach me the 'slider' pitch. He also reminded me of Alarid, except that Sanagorski always had the biggest chew in his mouth. He was patient and had a fabulous baseball mind.

King found me a job and an apartment, which was a customary deal for all Jayhawk players.

I worked as a bellhop at the Ramada Inn in downtown Wichita, which was a quick drive to Lawrence-Dumont Stadium, where we were going to play for the summer. It resulted in an exhausting season as we played nearly 60 games in three months in the muggy Midwestern heat.

THE SUNFLOWER STATE
GOT TO ME
Age 21

Aside from the climate, the travel was great. We played Kansas teams from Liberal, Hays and Hutchinson. There were games in the states of Nebraska, Iowa and Missouri. All this via a comfortable chartered bus that had all the amenities first class had to offer.

The talent pool was second to none. We had a pitching staff led by former Arkansas Razor-

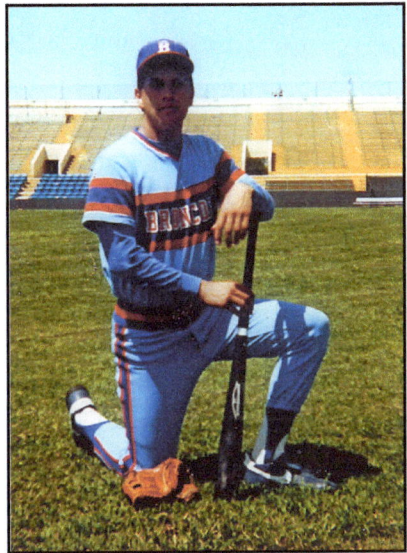

back, Kevin Campbell, who was drafted that summer by the Los Angeles Dodgers and made it all the way to the big leagues with the Oakland Athletics.

In the infield, we had a tall, skinny, slick shortstop out of Louisiana Tech named Jeff Richardson. He rose quickly through the minor leagues and became then-manager Pete Rose's starting shortstop with the Cincinnati Reds.

On the flipside, we had a diminutive right-handed pitcher by the name of Brian Corn, who was a 1986 preseason All-America pick as one of the country's finest prospects. Listed at 5-8, Corn threw well over 90 miles an hour, and defeated the Liberal Bee Jays— the National Baseball Congress World Series champion—several times that season.

Future New York Yankee manager, Joe Girardi, Todd Zeile, Jeff King, Matt Williams, Bo Jackson, Jack McDowell, and Greg Swindell, all joined Corn on the same All-America preseason team.

Bo Jackson, in fact, can be classified as one of the greatest all-time athletes. He and the others on this All-America team all made the Major League, but unfortunately for Corn, his small frame, mighty delivery, and all those innings against Liberal destroyed his arm. He tore his rotator cuff and never pitched again following the summer of '85.

All told, we had 16 players drafted to the majors from that squad alone. Yes, the Jayhawk League was a welcoming doormat to the pros, and its players came from all over.

The Jayhawk League was in mammoth proportions. It was a league among men. It was the kind of competition I imagined playing against. This was now the pinnacle of my young career.

I was employed primarily as a reliever in blowouts, where if we had a big lead, I'd be summoned for a mid-to-late-inning mop-up. At one point, I had nine appearances out of the bullpen, not allowing a hit, a walk or a runner to first base. It was nice to see the stat sheet display my miniscule ERA of 0.00.

By the end of July, the Broncos were playing in the NBC World Series as the host team. Once again, my number one fan, my mom, flew out to watch me. Although I never got to pitch in the WS, my mom sat amongst some 15,000 fans in amazement that her son was playing with the baseball elite.

Even if I was sitting on the bench, she was my proudest supporter.

In the WS, the Broncos surprised five-time NBC champion Alaska Goldpanners, 8-0, for what was the biggest upset of the tournament. But behind Texas Longhorn Swindell, who went 19-2 with a 1.67 ERA, the Liberal team swept through the competition.

Swindell, incidentally, was drafted in the first round of the draft the following year and made a rapid jump to the Cleveland Indians later that season. He pitched for 17 Major League seasons, winning 123 games that included one in the World Series while with the Arizona Diamond Backs.

As for myself, in all my years in baseball, I don't think I had seen better talent in a league than I did that summer in Wichita.

And when all was done that summer, after I had cherished all of the marvelous experience, I didn't want to return to Las Vegas and New Mexico High-lands. Seeing another part of this great country, I was again looking elsewhere.

Which is where coach Sanagorski fit in. He wanted me to become a Jet-setter, to play for Newman's Jets. With him coaxing me to join his Newman staff as the senior ace of the pitching staff, I was now at the fork in the road.

Stay or go? Leave the school that gave me my only full ride opportunity? Upset coach Marshall, who made all those countless calls around the country to plug his junior lefthander? Leave my family in the dust for a bigger prize? What about my education? Was it right to transfer as a senior?

Rod Tafoya and John Taylor

NOW PITCHING FOR THE JETS
Age 21

Newman. Yes or no?

And to be honest, I must admit that coach Sanagorski provided me with the answer. He answered my questions with ease and made me feel very comfortable in regard to making my own decision. I totally trusted him.

As I look back, I realize it was a no-brainer.

Sanagorski, himself, was a real winner. Enshrined in both the Wichita and Newman University Hall of Fame, he had won over 700 games. He was easy to become loyal to, easy to follow. He had character and pushed for higher education.

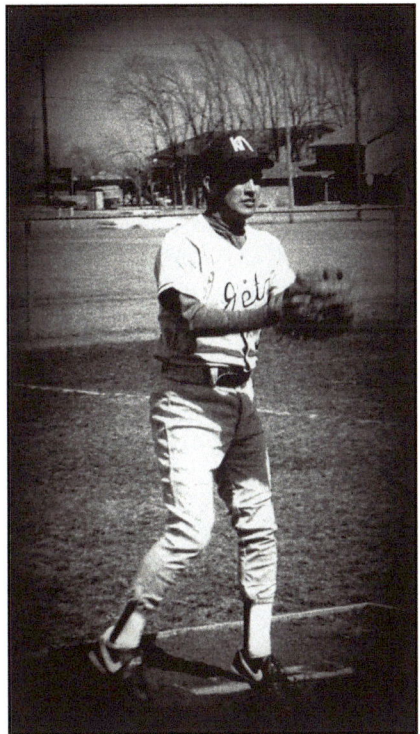

Newman was a private Catholic college with an impressive reputation for higher learning. It was an opportunity for me to get an even better education, as my marketing instructor and college advisor had just moved over from Harvard.

Things at Newman were now looking bright. And lucky for me, all my credits transferred over and I would be eligible as the season started in January of the next year.

I quickly found a small, affordable, one unit studio apartment located across from the school and a few hundred yards from the baseball complex. Life at Newman couldn't have been better and I assured my family of this.

My mom always told me that sometime in life, happiness is what matters most. To me, this was a wise decision.

In fall scrimmages I was lights out. My new surroundings were feeling very comfortable. I won against teams from Pratt Junior College and Fort Scott with ease.

As the winter months passed, I again sent out letters to all the major league clubs informing them of a new southpaw arriving on the Newman campus who threw a mid-80s fastball with excellent control.

I sent 30 letters in all, as this was my final attempt to get the scouts to come to the Wichita area. The only difference this time was that all the letters were signed by coach Sanagorski, except that he didn't know it.

Scouts made the scene, but one special one was James Terrell, who worked for the New York Mets. He contacted me and went to Oklahoma City to see me pitch. But I only lasted four innings against a tough opponent.

In the first few innings, I could see him taking notes and watching intently. By the fifth inning, he was nowhere in sight as the game fell away from us. To make matters worse, I was greeted by the lyrics of "Happy Trails to you, until we meet again," by the PA announcer, as Sanagorski arrived to take me off the mound.

Otherwise, the season came and went like a Jet flying at record speed. In my first four games, I was a perfect 4-0, with wins over Baker University, Bethany College, Arkansas Tech University, and Division One Kansas University.

It was that KU game in Lawrence, home of the Jayhawks that I was

most proud of. I shut them down, 10-0, allowing only six hits in going the distance, and giving the Jets their first victory over a D1 school in the program's nine-year history.

As the season was counting down, we were one of the favorites to win the District 7 tournament if we could get past rival Emporia State.

I started game one of the best-of-three playoff series against Washburn College in Wichita. Unfortunately, I got away to a shabby start. I gave up a bases-loaded walk to go with five- straight bases-on-balls to start the game, which infuriated Sanagorski as he yanked me out of the game with no out in the opening frame.

And if he was upset, I probably did him one better.

Figuring it was a mechanical failure in my wind-up being the cause of my rapid departure; I reached the dugout, saw a wheelbarrow in my reach and proceeded to toss it over the dugout in disgust.

Having seen this, Sanagorski summoned me to the dugout and sent me home. Another rapid departure on a day that didn't rank among my favorites.

Not knowing what my future was the next day, I headed to the public library, then to my apartment, locked the door, placed the phone on ringer, and read baseball and more baseball until I passed out.

That next morning I was back on the field in a nervous way, not knowing the consequences of my behavior the previous day. As I approached the dug-out, Sanagorski says, "Humm babe," as he tossed me the game ball. "Go get em".

Feeling better, I went out there and threw a complete nine-inning game as we turned back Washburn. It was Sanagorski who always believed in me, and there was a lesson to be learned.

Now pitching on three days' rest—the day after celebrating my 22nd birthday—I had to face the loaded Hornet lineup at a neutral site, Lawrence Dumont Stadium in Wichita. But because this was my home field with the Broncos the summer before, I knew I would feel very comfortable on the mound.

And when the dust settled, we came away with a 4-2 success over highly regarded Emporia State. I toiled for nine frames, gave up seven hits, struck out nine, and didn't walk a soul.

A few days later, we ended up in the championship of the District 7 playoffs and lost this time to the same Hornets.

This was the final chapter of my college baseball career.

Kansas Newman College 1986

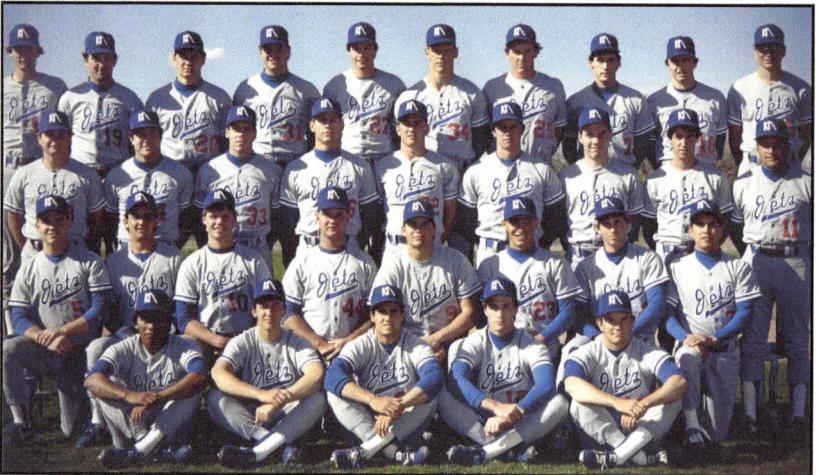

Photograph Courtesy of Gaines DuVall Sports Portraits

NERVOUS YES, BUT
NO TIME TO PANIC
Age 22

It was now due or die time for me. The future of my baseball career, my dreams and desires, all rested in the hands of the amateur draft.

Having been seen by the scouts, the games, the experiences, the travels, the trials and tribulations, it all broke down to the following summer months for me.

And so, still a full year away from graduating and with no eligibility left, I felt overwhelmed, nervous, and very vulnerable.

I also felt like pitching, and when I failed to hear from any of the Major League clubs by June, I decided to head west to Salt Lake City, Utah, for what I hoped would be an independent contract with the SLC Trappers of the Rookie Pioneer League.

But with hopes of signing the day I arrived, I was disappointed to hear that the club already had its roster completed. So I headed back to Santa Fe to make more calls. I was running on empty and running out of time. But it wasn't a time to panic.

It was a time to meet a young woman while attending the Blow Monkey's concert in Santa Fe. It was Emily, whom I had known for a brief time in high school, and we quickly hit it off. She was attractive, with the face of a model, with piercing green eyes.

She kept me from worrying about baseball that summer. While I worked out and held a part-time position as a lifeguard at one of the local swimming pools, Emily was a positive force in my life, as she rode horses and was a competitive person as well.

But baseball was numero uno, and much to my surprise, I received a phone call in July from Ozzie Alvarez, telling me that there was a roster spot open in some place known as La Liga Noroeste (AA Northwest League), although I didn't care where it was, I only wanted to play.

Much to my disbelief, it was a shot at playing for the AAA Pacific League's Naran-jeros de Hermosil-lo's farm team in Puerto Vallarta, (Jalisco, Mexico). Not knowing much about Puerto Vallarta, I quickly found out that if you were going to play baseball anywhere in the world, a beach port in a sunny, tourist-resort town would be unimaginable.

Later the next month, I received a call from the team owner, Jesus Barron, who owned a glass business there. He wanted to talk about offering me a contract if I was to make the team.

Enter mom again. She spoke directly to Barron, as her Spanish was excellent. Contingent on making the team, she had them promise to take care of my travel expenses, food (at a restaurant that would feed me three meals a day), a hotel that was suitable for my needs, and of course a contract that paid me enough to survive there for the season, which ran from September to January.

It was an exciting time for me as I carefully planned the rest of my summer. My arm had to be in the best condition if I was to make this team. The pressure was on me to gain the final roster spot on the Delfines (Dolphins). Again, my future as a baseball pitcher was depending on something.

I figured that my past experience in Pasteje was going to help. I knew there would be some familiar faces on this team.

As for Emily, after three short months together, it was time to say our goodbyes. She was off to UNM again and I was off to play more baseball.

It was a sad day as I left home for the airport. I didn't know how long this latest journey was going to last. I was also a bit frightened because I didn't speak the language very well. It was also a place I knew nothing about. It was more than 3,000 miles and I was already getting homesick.

The flight was a long one, first to Los Angeles, then to Puerto Vallarta. When we began to land, I could see the bay, the ocean, and the beach for miles. It was the first time I had ever seen an ocean. The excitement took over my sadness of missing Emily and my family. It was now time to take my traveling arm and make this roster.

It was mid-September in the tropics and the daytime heat was like 96 degrees. Dressed in my customary dark blue blazer and a tie, I grabbed a taxi and was off to take care of business.

The team's management staff had me report to one of those hole-in-the-wall hotels. But it did have air conditioning and that was all that mattered to me because it was hot.

That same day, they drove me straight to the stadium where I was to have my personal tryout. On the way, I took in magnificent views of the city. I saw antique cobblestoned streets, historic churches, beaches, and plenty of tourists from the states and elsewhere.

When we finally reached the stadium, I was greeted by my friend and catcher from Pasteje, Angel Navarro. He was a sight for sore eyes and I immediately felt at home with him being there. He gave me a wink and I knew he must have put in a good word for me.

It had also been awhile since I last pitched to Angel, so I wanted to show him all the improvements that my arm had made. It was, for me, a wonderful opportunity.

But all in all, it was just another day on the mound, to me my office.

LIVING IT UP IN
PUERTO VALLARTA
Age 22

So I headed to the mound, something I'd been doing for quite some time. I hummed the ball to Angel with all my might as newly appointed player-manager Oscar Mellado watched intently. He was a serious man with knowledge, as he knew pitching well and would double up as our right-handed reliever out of the bullpen when needed.

After I finished my repertoire of fastballs, sliders and off-speed curveballs, Mellado, Barron and three other co-owners of the team headed to the dugout while Angel and I reminisced. Angel gave me his customary wink of approval and the Vallarta brass walked slowly in my direction.

Not understanding a word they were saying, I was looking for a quick approval or disapproval, as I used a thumbs up or

down to get the decision from them. Yes? No? Did I make it?

Happily, I could tell by the smiles and handshakes that not only did I make the team, but I was being counted on as the number one starter in the rotation. It was a happy moment in my life.

It didn't take long for me to make a collect call to my mom and inform her of the wonderful news. I felt from that moment on that everything would now fall into place for me. I knew I was in good hands.

And I knew that beisbol in Puerto Vallarta was going to be beautiful. I now moved into the Marisol Hotel located on the beach. When that got boring, I headed to the more luxurious Torre de Oro.

I even had a restaurant that the team picked for me, except that the food was not what I expected and so I asked the guys if I could select another one, something like the "extranjero" (foreigner) could stomach.

Well, I myself found the perfect place around the corner that served seafood and all the American cuisine that I felt comfortable with. I knew that if my stomach was happy, my arm was going to pitch well over the course of the season.

As the season began, I didn't have much time on my hands. Since the games didn't start until 7 at night, I had much of the day to stroll around. My favorite thing to do was take in the sights at Mismaloya Beach, a site made famous by the late Elizabeth Taylor and the late Richard Burton, in the movie, "The Night of the Iguana."

I could take a "combi" (Volkswagen bus) to Mismaloya, rent an inner tube, and float into the ocean for hours for only $1.25 a day. But you have to remain alert, and I wasn't.

And so, on one particular occasion, I fell asleep in the inner tube and was awaken by a cruise ship that sounded its horn, as I had napped and sailed out to sea for more than a few miles. It took more than three hours to paddle back to shore, as I had accumulated nasty sunburn from my time at sea.

To pass my time on other days, I would hit many different resorts in Vallarta and pool hop. I must have visited at least a dozen resorts. Once I found a towel that belonged to the hotel, I was in. I looked like a traveling tourist.

But I also found out that most of these people knew who I was, and they were betting on my games when I pitched. Before my scheduled start, one resort owner would come over to me and offer to take me deep sea fishing on his boat if I won. Another time, an owner told me that if I won tonight, he'd take me for breakfast at his French restaurant.

I was called the "King of Vallarta" by one of my fellow Americans, Calvin Adams, who played for the Tepic team. He was one of my guests when they were in town to play us. He couldn't believe the lifestyle I was living.

I even had two maids that cleaned up every morning. They did my laundry and took care of most everything I needed. My hotel was beautiful to say the least. Open a curtain and you could see the view of the jungle, open another and you would get a view of the city, and open another and see a magnificent view of the Pacific Ocean.

During the playoffs of that year, Emily decided to visit me, so she took a leave from college, hopped on a plane, and surprised me. She spent several weeks there, as I was forced to bring her along on a two-week long road trip after I convinced the team owners to bring her along because I couldn't possibly think of leaving her behind in Vallarta by herself.

Emily was probably the first North American female to ever ride on a road trip through Mexico with a team of beisbol players.

And I had a very good season on the mound, winning 10 games and being named to the All-Star team. Plus, I had already traveled the circuit to places like Compostela, Guadalajara, Tepic, Acaponeta, Tecuala, Santiago, and Tuxpan.

On one particular bus trip, I had the driver stop several times so that I could climb a tree and pick bananas, mangos and coconuts. After my 10th victory, I had my own seat on the bus with my own personal cooler with my favorite beverage. Life on the road was great.

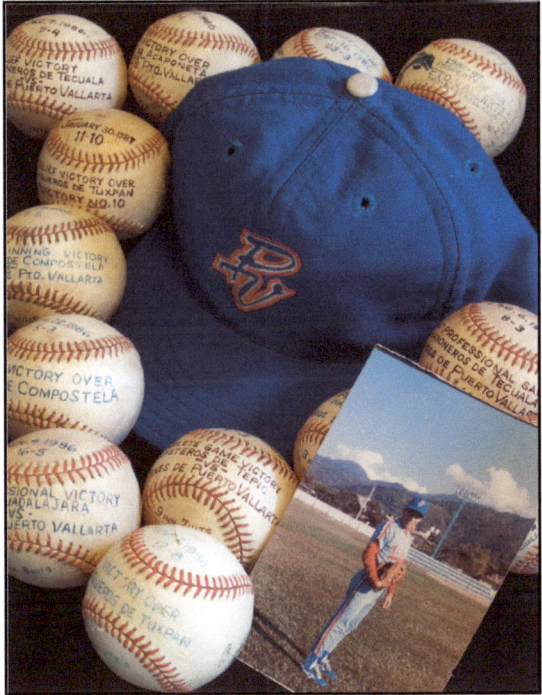

Photograph by Nick Sedillos

Then, as the season ended, my contract was sold to the Mexico City Diablos Rojos of the AAA Mexican

League, where I would join them in Durango for spring training in February.

YUP, ME
AND
JOHN WAYNE SLEPT HERE
Ages 22-23

Durango, the place that John Wayne made famous. He was a cowboy, so was I when I wore the uniform of NMHU.

It was in the northern part of the country. It was where I had to report for spring training after the Mexico City Diablos Rojos selected my contract rights during the winter league.

Of course I still had hopes of making the big club and perhaps making what I called a career in the Mexican League.

Back home, my dad had now taken an unanticipated interest in my baseball career. He offered to give me a ride to the airport in Albuquerque. From there, I was going to catch a quick flight to Juarez on Aero Mexico. There, I would

board a direct flight to Durango and join the organization for a month of spring training.

But first dad would come to my rescue. When I said goodbye to him, I had an unexpected emergency as I ripped my luggage zipper. Dad was calm, told me not to worry, went to the gift shop and bought me a bright red duffel bag, albeit to matching my team's colors.

Once 'mad' dad, he was now dad in the pinch as he was there to drive me to the airport and there to replace my broken luggage zipper.

I arrived in Durango later that day and checked into the Hotel Presidente, where I was one of over 70 baseball players of the Diablos' organization. They were known as the New York Yankees of the Mexican League for their long tradition of winning and for players that they signed.

They had an all-star list. Home run hitter Nelson Barreras, a Hall of Famer who hit 455 homers to clip Espino's career mark of 453, was our third baseman. There was major league reliever, Salome Barrojas, who pitched for the White Sox, Mariners and Phillies.

We also had our list of gringos. John Martin, a journeyman left-handed pitcher, had hurled for the World Champion St. Louis Cardinals in the early 80s, and Dave Schuler, a major league pitcher for the Atlanta Braves.

The Diablos were loaded.

I wasn't sure what my reason for being there was, but anytime I dressed in the teams' uniform, I always thought I had a chance.

We were managed by Benjamin "Cananea" Reyes, who served major league time as a coach for the Seattle Mariners, and who had a solid reputation as a coach. I was also encouraged to learn that he had no problem giving work to young pitchers.

I threw relief in several games against Saltillo and the Mexico City Tigres. I won my first game in what I thought was the most beautiful city on earth, Salamanca, Guanajuato.

I even won praise from Martin and Schuler, who thought from what they had seen; I had a good chance of making the team. It was Martin who I spent most of the time with, dining together at the local John Wayne restaurant, and him teaching me what he had learned as a "big leaguer."

As the team made its way to Mexico City for the start of the season, we played in various states in Central Mexico. We passed through Guanajuato and Leon, an area that I fell in love with. It reminded me of Santa Fe.

At the Hotel Saratoga in Mexico City, I had my own room, which was rather peculiar to me. The next day, I was rooming with center fielder Rufino Linares, a Dominican ex-major leaguer who had just signed with the team.

This meant only one thing to me. The league had a rule on how many "estranjeros" it could keep, as in a limit of four. With Jesse Baez, our starting catcher, Martin, Schuler, and now Linares, I was the fifth and odd man out.

To make matters worse, as we checked out of the hotel and headed to the stadium (Parque Seguro Social), I took a cab with all my packed luggage for the summer, as I was instructed to do so by the team.

Once I arrived there, I was amazed by not only the size of the city (26 million), but the number of lanes in front of the stadium, (which would pack in a crowd of 30,000, a sellout).

There must have been at least seven lanes of traffic, as my "crooked cabbie" dropped me off in front of the entrance gates to the sold-out stadium.

In a flash, as I got out of the cab, he horribly drove off into the mixed lanes of traffic, and I did not know if his car was red, blue, green or yellow, as it all happened so fast. Simply put, I was caught off guard and robbed.

All of my personal belongings were being driven away. My uniform, spikes, glove, identification, money, clothes, everything gone in an instant.

In total disbelief, I waited for him, the driver, for about an hour, thinking that he must have panicked with the rush hour traffic. But he never returned. And all I had was the suit on my back, feeling empty, lonely, and angry!

To make matters worse, the organization sent manager Alberto Joachin to pick me up that night. I was to be his 'ace' for the Cocoateros de Comalcalco, which was located in the Gulf of Mexico in the state of Tabasco.

Worse, I was being sent down to the 'farm', where all the 18-23 year olds went to get more seasoning. La Liga Tabasquena, as it was referred to, was the "mosquito league."

Now, feeling shattered, tired, and lost, I had to accompany Joachin, who was dragging me on a bus to Tabasco, some 1,300 miles away.

Having now encountered my first experience with tough times, all I wanted to do was go home to New Mexico.

NO VISA, NO LICENSE, NO PASSPORT
Age 23

First I had to have a tug-of-war. Alberto Joachin versus my desire to return to New Mexico, because *this* Mexico was feeling 'old' to me.

As far as Joachin goes, it was the first time in my life that I felt what it was like to be owned. Even as he tried his best to console me, I was now the property of the Diablos and they tracked my every move.

On the way there, Joachin made attempts to take my mind off of things. We stopped in Cordoba, where he got us a motel room. He lent me some of his sweats, shoes and T-shirt, took me to a field and made me run for hours.

He was a disciplinarian and he needed me in the right frame of mind as my new season began the following week. His mission that early spring was to get me back to the AAA Mexican League.

Simply put, we were both on a mission.

My thoughts now were to make a collect call to mom and tell her the news. But when I asked her to get me out of this country, she instead told me not to worry and that both Joachin and the Diablos would take care of me.

As for the stolen clothes and material goods that I let her know about, she said they could all be replaced. She told me that she had a new Spiegel credit card and would take care of the clothes that I lost.

That was how special my mom was. She advised me not to come home and to continue following my dreams.

"Keep fighting, keep a positive attitude, and good things will follow," I remember her saying.

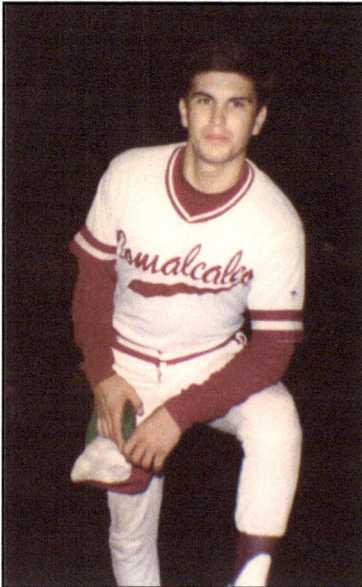

In my first week in Comalcalco, I had wild experiences.

There was the time I was running poles in the outfield and was chased by a huge iguana, only to be rescued by five young boys who clubbed and killed it, then being ridiculed by my rescue team. Or the night when I looked down at my white baseball pants to see a string of red dots all over my legs, being eaten alive by the giant mosquitos they called "zancudos."

But it was the 117 degrees heat that I couldn't bare the most. Now I know where they got the name for Tabasco sauce.

I traveled to some odd, yet exciting places that spring. There was Paraiso, Agua Dulce, Huimanguillo and Jalpa. All of these sites were in Veracruz and Tabasco. I even took a few days off to see the Mayan Pyramids in Palenque, Chiapas. It was a learning education to see the jungle, the ocean, all the beautiful beaches, and all that the Gulf of Mexico had to offer.

That season I went 5-5 for a mediocre team. The campaign ended in June and I was ready to hop a plane and head home after an exhausting nine months of baseball. As I said my goodbyes, Joachin came to my hotel room with some unexpected, yet exciting news.

In his hand, Joachin held a telegram that read: "You made it! You and Jorge Morfin have been optioned to the Aguascalientes Rieleros (Railroad Workers) of the AAA Mexican League. You have two days to get to Aguascalientes by bus ... Congratulations!!!"

Morfin and I had been friends since our time in Pasteje together. Once we arrived, the Rieleros didn't waste any time getting us in a game. I was primarily used as a left-handed relief specialist out of the bullpen.

Both of our coaches were experienced. Our manager, Kaliman Robles, played for the Los Angeles Dodgers and Baltimore Orioles in the early to mid-1970s, as did my pitching coach, Jose Pena, who pitched for the Dodgers and Cincinnati Reds. Both had been inducted into the Mexican Hall of Fame.

We also had a reliable reliever in Warren Brusstar, who pitched for the Philadelphia Phillies' World Series champion in 1980. He was a journeyman pitcher who loved to take the mound and wasn't ready to hang up his spikes yet. He was great to be around, as he was an experienced big leaguer on and off the field.

Another one of our leaders was journeyman utility infielder, Mario Mendoza, who played for the Seattle Mariners and Pittsburgh Pirates. He was known as a slick-fielding shortstop who couldn't hit more than .200, so he was forever known as the "Mendoza Line."

All in all, I made eight appearances that summer. Of the eight games, three were starts, including one at home against the heavy-hitting Tecos de Nuevo Laredo, another at home against the Los Bravos de Leon, and one away against the Sultanes de Monterrey.

Although my experience was great, I was often overmatched by the league's abundance of talent. When I went against Jesus Sommers, the only player in the league to knock out over 3,000 career hits, he blasted an opposite field line drive off me that shot out of the stadium like a missile in seconds.

After my eighth appearance, I was invited to have dinner with the team's general manager, who spoke in broken English when he informed me that I wasn't getting the job done, and that my time in the Mexican League was done, and that he wished me well in my future endeavors.

He also mentioned that the team was heading north on a road trip and would drop me off as close to Aguascalientes as they could, so I could move out of my hotel, collect my final paycheck, and fly home.

I was now set to leave Mexico with a sense of urgency as the summer had its ups and downs. But not so fast I thought. I had no visa, no license or a passport to prove my identity. I didn't know if I was ever going to make it out of this country.

SCARY, BUT BACK IN THE USA
Age 25

And so, as the team bus dropped me off on the side of the road that early morning, near the city of Aguascalientes, I was sincerely frightened and thought this might be some kind of joke or prank.

Except the reality was that this wasn't a prank, not even a joke.

No, it was a 'kind' gesture by the Mexican League team to drop me off in the darkness on a deserted highway to nowhere. I could hear the coyotes howling in the distance, so I knew what to do best ... pray.

As the team drove off in the chartered team bus, I was left in a fog of dust. As I looked around, there wasn't any sign of life, although I did see a light in the distance coming from a group of trees one hundred feet away.

It was a taxicab. The driver flicked his bright lights at me, picked me up and drove me to Aguascalientes. I couldn't have been happier, except I wasn't overjoyed at the overall picture.

The next day I met with team president Moi Camacho, who handed me my final check and an airplane ticket to Albuquerque. He thanked me for my services on the mound and offered to help me find another job if he could.

Unfortunately, Camacho didn't tell me that there was no airport out of Aguascalientes. Thus, it was now up to me to get to Guadalajara, where I could take a direct flight to Houston and then to Albuquerque, where I would hope to arrive home safely.

Or so I thought.

Finding my way to Guadalajara wasn't going to be an easy task. The flight I needed was departing at 6 p.m. Now it's 11 in the morning as I headed to the bus depot to board a Tres Estrellas bus liner that would get me to Guadalajara by 5:30 p.m.

Once on the bus, I gave the bus driver my belt, shoes, and jacket in exchange for a faster bus ride. If I was to miss that flight, I wouldn't get home, so I began giving him everything that I had.

But it wasn't working because he had other stops and wasn't moving fast enough for me. So after a bizarre journey, he, too, dropped me off on the side of the road and I quickly stopped a taxicab and we sped at speeds of over 100 mph to race me to the airport.

I made it with 10 minutes to spare.

In a panic, I asked the airlines personnel to please page the pilot of the plane, who I figured could get me on his plane as I had no identity. After a few phone calls, I was secured in my seat and heading to the good old USA.

After a brief winter gig in Southern California with the Houston Astros franchise, I was now out of options, so I took my safest bet at the time.

I enrolled back at Newman University, where I became coach Sanagorski's pitching coach. Back on scholarship for what were my final credit hours, I became a student again with the hopes and dreams of pitching yet one more time as a professional.

While at my apartment one night, I received a phone call from Mal Fichman, the coach for the Class A Northwest League Boise Hawks. The Hawks operated as an independently owned club and could find the nation's best pro talent through their invitation-only baseball tryout camps.

Following several conversations with Fichman, I flew to Ontario, Calif., where I would be one of over

100 invitation-only campers vying for a spot on the Hawks' roster.

Two days of scoreless pitching no doubt impressed Fichman, and he tendered me a contract. In an instant, I was again a pro player.

Heading back to Newman, I was on cloud nine. At last my visions of playing pro ball in the states were going to be fulfilled.

Fichman, to me, was the "man." He had a great reputation for finding hidden talent throughout the country. It was he who put these tryout camps together, where he could find a needle in a haystack or a diamond in the rough.

I'm thinking I was Fichman's diamond in the rough and was being counted on as his fifth starter. The Northwest League was a tough short season. It was where major league organizations sent their top high school and/or college prospects for minor league seasoning.

So with only two months of college remaining, I used the Newman baseball program to round me into shape for the upcoming season that began in June.

Now, as my family was preparing to see me graduate from college in late May, it was only interrupted by a drive to Boise, where I had to report for pitching duty, which took precedent over the graduation exercises.

As disappointed as my family was that there wasn't to be a graduation ceremony to attend, my mom was ecstatic that I was playing pro ball again and my dad was overjoyed that I was going to receive my college diploma.

It was wonderful to have a supporter in each corner.

With my diploma now in hand, my family presented me with a brand new Corsica. My dad came through with a $1,500 cashier's check to help pay for my summer's rent, so that, he said, I could concentrate on my pitching.

I set off to Boise that summer with relief. My mom was always there for me, but my dad went 24 years before providing me with his support and blessing.

PLAYING PRO BALL PAINTED A PRETTY PICTURE
Ages 23-25

It took all of two days of traveling to arrive in Boise, where I was now a college grad headed to pitch professional baseball.

I couldn't have been prouder.

My journey as a left-handed pitcher had taken me to more places than I had ever dreamed about, and I was being heavily counted on for all my experience. After all, it was experience that won games, and Mal Fichman knew my history on the hill.

I had traveled so much in Mexico, I sometimes felt like a south-of-the-border citizen.

Now I was back in my native land. No language barrier, no issues with the cuisine, and I was with a group of teammates who all felt they had something to prove.

The summer started slow as I did my best to get acclimated to professional baseball in the states. The travel was just as weary, but there weren't to be any excuses.

It was a roster of has-been, washed-up journey-men minor leaguers and organizational cast-offs. We set high standards to beat all our competition. We were an older group.

With the league starting in mid-June, they referred to it as a 'short season,' as we played 75 games in 78 days.

We did plenty of traveling through the good old USA's northwest. It was a summer of bus rides to Oregon's Eugene, Salem, Medford and Bend, as well as to Washington's Bellingham, Everett and Spokane.

The NW was beautiful country with a wide array of rivers, lakes and lush green mountains. It had to be one of the prettiest places on the planet.

The talent around the league was also impressive.

We had over 25 players who made it to the major leagues. Among them were Hall of Fame catcher Mike

Piazza and outfielder/DH Tim Salmon, who starred for the Los Angeles Angels.

As for myself, judging by the competiveness of this pro league, it was perhaps my finest season on the mound. I started nine of a dozen games. I compiled a 3-4 won-lost record, but I also came away with a 3.26 earned run average in 47 innings of pitching.

It was a summer where I received my first professional baseball card, a humbling experience to this day. It was a culmination of all the hard work I had put into the sport, and it was finally paying off.

My passion was still living in the core!

Photograph by Nick Sedillos

THE EMERALD SKY BROUGHT ME TIME
Age 25

Boise, Boise, Idaho, where they grow potatoes and where its celebrated Boise State football team plays its home games on *blue turf*.

Except that we were now hitting the road. We bused some 14 hours through the night after playing the Los Angeles Dodgers' farm team, the Salem Dodgers, the previous night.

I remember rolling into the city of Eugene, Ore., for the first time in the summer of '89. We were going up against the Eugene Emeralds, the Kansas City Royals' Northwest League entry, in a five-game series.

And a worthy note was that I had never before seen the color of emerald green that I viewed from the bus. I thought this had to be one of the most beautiful places on earth. I witnessed the picturesque rivers, mountains, and rolling hills and the color of emerald green was prominent through the region.

I imaged that the rainfall here must be consistent in order to have trees so green and lush. Deep down in the bottom of my mind I thought that someday I'll live right in Eugene and make a new life for myself.

It was a place that felt just right for me as the team began to settle in the hotel that morning. After a morning breakfast there, I strolled to downtown Eugene to find a myriad of little shops and restaurants that I would later visit.

The days just appeared to go so fast, so usually I would wake up early, head outdoors, and make my way around to find special interests. Local museums, coffee shops, and restaurants were always on the top of my list.

By now it was 1 in the afternoon and our chartered bus was about ready to head to the ballpark. We didn't play until 7 that night, but we wanted to get there for a 1:30 practice.

We were playing at aging Civic Stadium, built some 50 years ago. I especially liked the older stadiums because of the grandstand area and the advertisements on the outfield fences and the areas around them.

It had that old-time feeling. It was a ballpark with the smell of hot dogs and hamburgers roasting on the grill, and drink-up time at the newly renovated beer garden.

The team was owned by the husband and wife team of Bob and Eileen Beban. They were a charming couple with tons of energy and passion for the game of baseball. They knew how to put on a great show by offering an affordable venue tied to a warm family environment for entertainment.

On our side of the fence, Mal Fichman was the Boise manager and we had a number of run-ins. The first came in an embarrassing incident. It was on the road trips prior to the Eugene game that I had been collecting batting practice balls from every game and tossing them in my bag.

Before long, more of the players gathered up practice balls and stuck them in their bags. This was all a violation of team policy, and I'm certain, league policy.

One time before a game, Fichman ordered a search to check every team member's bag for stolen baseballs. Unfortunately, my bag of balls greatly outnumbered the others, meaning that I was to be disciplined for sure.

And so, after an uneventful meeting with Fichman, he told me that if he ever again caught me stealing balls from other organizations, he would release me and make sure that all the newspapers in New Mexico would hear about it.

Fichman didn't stop there. He was a disciplinarian who I highly respected, and the next day decided to suspend me for my next start against the Salem Dodgers. On the other hand, I was thankful that I was still on the team. I had to move on.

But I also felt some embarrassment going to Salem, where we played at Chemekeda Field, and I was looking forward to pitching to Mike Piazza, the Dodgers' slugging catcher who was tearing up the league that summer.

By my next time on the hill—game five versus Eugene—I was deep in the zone and looking at charts of my assignment. I tried to listen to some music to relax, and then started to dress in my uniform.

My clothes were neatly hung in my locker with black Nike spikes freshly painted and polished by our 13-year-old clubhouse boy named Scooter, whom we decided to take on the road.

As I started my wind sprints in the outfield, I felt strong and comfortable. We had dropped four-straight here in Eugene, and at the end of four innings, we were locked in a scoreless tie. I had seven strikeouts in a row and no walks.

But I was feeling good, so locked in that I didn't even notice the home fans cheering for a sweep. Still in a scoreless tie going into the sixth inning, I had only scattered three hits. In the seventh, we broke loose for a 5-0 lead and Fichman gave me a congratulatory pat on the back and told me it was a good job.

I knew I was now in the good graces of Fichman. He even tossed the baseball to me.

I had struck out 10, did not allow a pass, and held all-league outfielder and 2011 New York Yankee hitting instructor Kevin Long to 0-for-4, which included a strikeout. We held on for the win and Fichman noted later that I had made 97 pitches in seven innings, a big improvement over my last time out.

The best part was what occurred in our visitor's locker room after the final out. There was pure jubilation. You could hear laughter in the shower and guys joking around. That's what winning does for a team, especially since we avoided being swept.

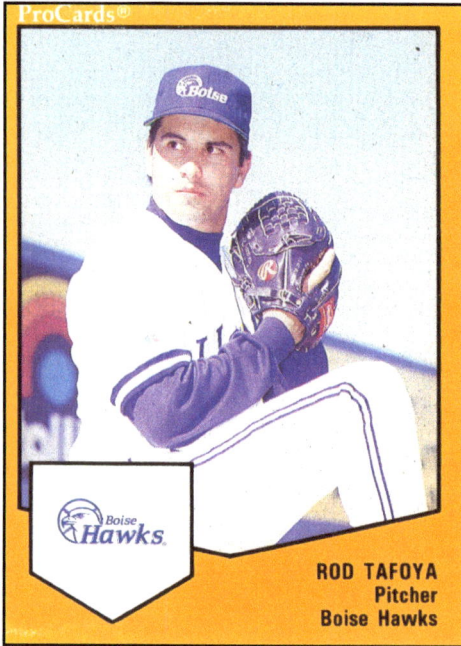

For me, I knew at this point that I was going to be a professional pitcher for at least one more start.

It was also a magical night that I wished would never end, and I was one lucky star shining in an emerald sky.

"TAFOYA, I'M SORRY, BUT YOU'RE DONE"
Ages 25-26

With all these neat things happening in the USA, I still had Mexico on my mind. No doubt the reason was that I loved to pitch. Here, there or anywhere.

And so after my first season in Boise, I was back at my old stomping grounds, the Liga Noroeste in the state of Sinaloa. I was now a member of the Pescadores (Fishermen) de Esquinapa, a farm club of the Mexico City Diablos Rojos.

Needing more work on my slider pitch, I took a winter job to hone my skills at yet another shot of making it in the big leagues.

I roomed with future Albuquerque Isotope manager Lorenzo Bundy, a fan favorite and home run hitter from the Pirates' organization who made a living in Mexico.

In my first game there while pitching to former Dodger Lemmie Miller, I uncorked an 80 mph hard slider to strike him out. In the process, though, I heard my elbow pop. This was followed by a warm, tingling sensation, where I lost all feeling of the ball in my hand.

In my words, I was done! Finished!

It took a month before the team would release me. It was in favor of me staying in Mexico, getting surgery, and rehabbing for the summer season. It had their own way of dealing with things. After all, I was its property and they wanted it done their way.

But I managed to find my way back to Santa Fe. There, I met with surgeon Robert Lipscomb, who diagnosed me with an avulsion. This is where the tendon in the elbow rips off of the bone. Being rather painful and career threatening, we opted to place my left arm in a cast for six months.

At the end of December, I received a phone call from Mal Fichman saying he was moving to the New York-Penn League to manage the upstart Erie Sailors, another independent team.

By now, my relationship with Fichman was very positive and he signed me on the spot as the team's fifth man in the rotation.

With time on my side, I just waited for the injury to heal.

By April, the cast was removed and the arm was going through the rigors of therapy. I knew I wasn't ready, but I did have a contract and had to report to Erie by mid-June.

This trip was a long haul. I was now driving to Pennsylvania, where I would appear in only three games as part of the Sailors' rotation. After winning my first start over the Jamestown Expos, five days later I was called on to pitch against St. Catherine's Blue Jays, who had future major league slugger Carlos Delgado in the lineup.

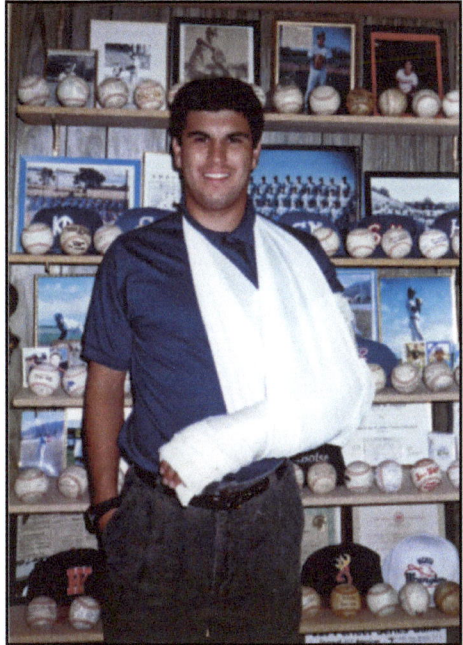

After losing a tense, close game to the Blue Jays, I could feel the tendon in my elbow ready to snap again. I feared for my life. I was in so much pain I wasn't sure I could pitch competitively again.

Following a trip to Welland, Ontario, the team headed back to Erie, where I was to start against the

Hamilton Cardinals. After a hard shellacking, I hit the showers early and was later called into Fichman's office.

"Tafoya," he said, "I'm sorry, but you're done."

There was nothing else to say. To me, it was like the shortest release job in the history of baseball. But don't blame Fichman, for he did what he had to do. He needed a live arm and mine was dying.

Years later I would run into Fichman in Arizona. He asked me if I still had the baseball card collection. He chuckled and told one of his San Diego Padres scouts that I would bring the cards on the bus and read them all night during the bus ride.

I later joined Fichman as a scout for the Padres years later. We had forged a bond that was fostered in Wichita when he invited me to a tryout camp.

By now, baseball was a thing of the past for me. I had some inner anger issues with the sport as it left me high and dry.

After three years, I relocated to the northwest to recover some of my lost dreams and used my degree to get my initial job as a banker. It was there that one spring that I decided to play catch with a youngster whom I had met at the bank.

It was in Eugene, Ore., and I found that my love and passion for the game of baseball never went away. With no pain in my arm now, I began to envision the future and conjured up thoughts of one day pitching again.

I found a local team in Eugene called the Rockies. I attended a few practice sessions and found myself right where I left off. In my mind, I was a pitcher once more.

Enter the men's senior baseball league (MSBL) and men's adult baseball league (MABL), a national organization in the United States with 325 affiliates, 3,200 teams, and 45,000 members who play organized amateur ball in local leagues, 30 regional tournaments and six national tourneys.

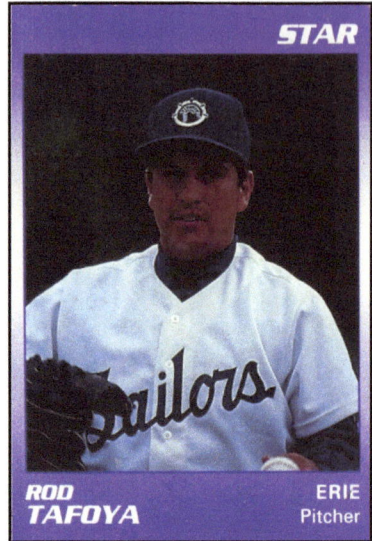

I had now found a home in a league where I felt I belonged; even if it was considered a recreational league. In the next three seasons, I won 37 games and lost only three. People would come up to me and ask why I wasn't pitching professionally.

Feeling the passion that never left me, I hooked on with the Portland Twins and made the MSBL World Series in Phoenix that year.

From there, I moved back to Santa Fe and became a vice president of a local bank. So here I was, 33 years old and a bank officer starting what was my new life.

But what about my old life as a baseball pitcher?

BACK IN MEXICO WITH MOM THIS TIME AND STILL PITCHING AT THE AGE OF 39
Ages 33-39

One week. That's all it took for me to figure out what I wanted out of my life.

Until now, I was always one to listen and obey my family's wishes.

And so I upset nearly everyone in my family with my decision to call Jack Uhey, one of my teammates in Portland who was a fellow pitcher/journeyman minor leaguer for several years.

He was now a regional scout for the California Angels. I still had the business card he gave me when he told me to let him know if I'm still interested in pitching professionally.

So I contacted Uhey, who had strong ties to every league in America, including the Northern League that played independent ball. He said, let's do it.

When I called my boss at the bank to tell him of my decision, he came up with a brilliant plan where I could take a sabbatical leave for up to five months. I knew my family would agree to this as long as I had my bank job back when I returned.

From then on, I was on a personal quest to make it and show all those with inner passion, that no matter your age, no matter what obstacles are in the way, if you follow your heart, you can become whatever it is you want to be.

My next move was to introduce myself to Carl Miller, who was the 1976 USA Summer Olympic Team weightlifting coach in Montreal. He had a gymnasium near my home in

Santa Fe and I wanted his expertise, wisdom and passion to fuel my fire.

It was Miller who chiseled my body in less than six months. Losing 25 pounds and adding five miles to my fastball, I wasn't your ordinary 33-year-old.

Now I booked a flight to Malibu, Calif., where the tryout arranged by Uhey was being held. I recognized a few faces, but the majority of the players were like 10 plus years younger.

Right away the odds were against me. The leader of the camp informed me that guys don't start careers at my age, they end them. I let it glance off of me. I only wanted to pitch and prove I belong.

I threw well and retired every batter I faced.

One of the majority owners of the Sioux Falls Explorers, Bill Pereier, came over to say hello. He was one of the principal owners in Boise when I played there. He came right to the point, telling me that he'd love to have me, but when he can get the same out of a 20-year-old.

End of conversation.

The next day, another ex-Boise Hawk stepped onto the field. Player-manager Tommy Griffin, a former teammate of mine back in 1989, was coaching in the Prairie League. His team, the Regina Cyclones, were on the lookout for "strays", that were available from the camp.

Griffin immediately called me and offered me a contract. It arrived just in time for my birthday, May 7.

In early June, my healed-up arm and my new chiseled body packed up in my Saab convertible for a three-day journey to Regina, Saskatchewan, Canada, for one last hurrah.

As the old man of the team, many of the guys questioned my existence. They wanted to know why the general manager is always following us around at night. That's not the GM, one said, that's our fifth starting pitcher.

Being a banker, I already had my own sense of style. I wore freshly starched shirts, tasseled loafers, and sports jackets. Driving a sporty convertible and always looking sharp, I guess I looked the part of the team's GM.

This time around I took it all in, as if this would be my last time as a professional. I led the team with six wins and I praised our run support. We reached the championship series, but didn't win once in the best-of-three against the Mallard Ducks of Minot.

The Prairie League was something new for me.

There were nice places like Brandon, Manitoba, Moose Jaw, Saskatoon (City of Bridges), Minot, Grand Forks, Southern Minnie (Austin, Minn.), the home of Hormel Foods and Spam, and Aberdeen, where legendary Satchel Paige won 29 games one summer.

I saw many things, fished for northern pike, and saw the Northern Lights dancing in the sky.

With every end, there's a new beginning. For me, my new beginning was the MSBL. I now dreamed up new things and new places to pitch.

I wondered how many teams could I pitch for? How many championship rings could I win? The thoughts were endless.

By the start of the MSBL World Series in Phoenix in mid-October, I was now pitching for the DeMarini Giants out of Portland. When we beat a team from Sonoma County, 27-7, it would be my 100th victory in the MSBL.

A few years later, in March of 2004, I found myself pitching back in Mexico, in the state of Chihuahua, for a team out of Casas Grandes. I had come full circle, for I had pitched on these same fields some 20 years ago.

I even had the courage to bring my surprised mom along and she witnessed the first championship for Casas Grandes since 1977. And with me starting the title game at the ripe old age of 39 was indeed an accomplishment and a double treat for my mom.

The following season, I signed what would be my final pro contract. It was with the Peidras Negras Astros and I went 4-0, but it wasn't the games that amazed people, it was the way I traveled.

TOO MUCH FOR
THE TRAVELING MAN
Age 40

I felt like a traveling salesman with a passion for baseball.

To Mexico, back to Albuquerque, home to Santa Fe. Then toss in the bus rides to the playing fields.

Yes, it became much too much.

To put this into gear, it took me over 10 hours to get to the border city of Piedras Negras. Nearly two hours south of San Antonio, Tex., it was quite a long haul from Santa Fe.

And once I reached the border bridge, I phoned "El Knocke", a former Golden Gloves boxer and chief of police for the city of Piedras Negras. His namesake was given to him for the great TKO (technical knock-out) punch he packed in the ring.

After all, it was his younger brother, Raul Avila, who I played for in Santa Fe, who gave me a shot at playing again in Mexico. He arranged for a tryout, introduced me long distance to El Knocke, who said he would always take care of me while in Mexico.

Once I phoned El Knocke, he arrived in his fancy patrol car and escorted me in my new BMW to the gates of the hotel parking lot. He made sure I got into my room, and the following day he would make sure that I arrived at the ballpark safely.

One day while driving in the squad car with him, he received a call on his receiver and we engaged in a wild high speed chase in the city in chase of a would-be narcotics bust. In the back seat, I could only hope of getting out alive, as I bounced around like a rubber ball.

After the assailant was caught and surrounded by a squadron of police cars, I was left in amazement in the back seat, wondering what did I get myself into?

Then again, life with El Knocke was interesting to say the least, and I always felt safe. At least that's what I told myself.

Flying solo from Piedras Negras back to Santa Fe was always the difficult part of the journey. After an 11 a.m. game on Sunday, I would be on the road by 5 p.m. and would pull into Albuquerque around 5 in the morning on Monday, just in time to head for my bank's bathroom where I would take a sponge bath in the sink.

I was now a vice president with Compass Bank in the state's largest city. By 6 a.m., I was sitting in my office in a coordinated suit looking the part of my profession, a banker. I did this for two straight years and it wore me down.

As much as I loved baseball, travel, and the money I earned, I had to stop for fear of my life.

My life? Well, a day that I had returned from Mexico still tired from having little rest, I was driving to Santa Fe from my position at the bank when I almost lost 'it' as my BMW swerved into the interstates median after I must have dozed off for a few seconds.

As important as baseball was to me, that was my last straw of traveling back-and-forth south of the border.

THIS LEFTY IS STILL IN QUEST OF 300 ... BY THE AGE OF 50 AT LEAST!

Ages 43-46

Photograph by Nick Sedillos

Three hundred was my number. That's how many games I wanted to win. So now it was summer of 2011 and I had reached 260, and with already 17 years of 15 wins, I would need three seasons of 15 to reach the milestone, my personal milestone.

To reach back, it was in 2007 that I won my 200th game with a quick 10-run rule romp over the Nationals. Germaine Casey, a member of the Albuquerque police force, was one of my teammates, a special one. Later that summer, officer Casey succumbed to injuries sustained in a motorcycle accident providing an escort for President George W. Bush. The accident occurred as the motorcade returned to Kirkland Air Force Base in Albuquerque.

As the motorcade rounded a curve, Casey's motorcycle left the roadway and struck a tree. He was treated by medical personnel on the scene and then transferred to the University of New Mexico Hospital, where he died.

This was truly sad. As Casey at the bat, he was one of the nation's most feared amateur hitters. He took me along on one of his trips to Arizona as we both shared the same passion for the game. Me a banker and he a law enforcement officer.

We shared a bond. We traveled to other places like Florida, Alabama and Georgia. We both took almost five weeks of paid vacation from work to play baseball all over the land. I'll never forget Casey.

So now, in respect to him, I had yet another reason to continue pitching. Age was just a number now.

And as many ridiculed my dream to reach 300, saying it was nothing more than recreational ball, many never knew of my story and the passion that drove me to this.

They never knew of how, at age 2, my brother Jack had tied my right arm behind my back, how he had this plan to make me into a left-handed athlete.

They never knew of all the traveling I did, the countries I competed in, the language barriers I had to face, the strange lands, the states I played in, airline flights to places unknown, stranded in a foreign country, teammates and more teammates ... it would take a book to tell all this.

Only my family knew of my history on the hill. The only thing they didn't know about was this book—**AGELESS ARM**. This would be my surprise gift to them.

My brother **Jack** retired from the State of New Mexico where he was a budget analyst.

Most of his time is spent attending my games with my mom. They try to attend most weekend games, and Jack still tracks all my pitching statistics and they are then recorded on each game ball for preservation. He has done this for 18-plus years that I hurled in the MSBL/MABL, and has rarely missed a game.

My **dad** passed away in October of 1998 at the age of 81. He suffered a heart attack and then a stroke. But he passed knowing that I had a college degree and was still pitching.

And my **mom**, who joined me in Mexico, well, I wish she had a safer stay. Alas, on my last road trip that season, she took a nasty step.

After my fourth win and final game, I noticed a commotion around my mom near the team's dugout. She had tripped in her high heels, apparently over a water hose that was running through a graveled area.

As I feared the worst, I hauled her into the car and headed back to my hotel. I knew better not to take her to a Mexican hospital, so I made the decision to make her feel as comfortable as I could and get her home to Santa Fe ASAP.

We arrived there early the next morning and I called my sister. The following day, my mom had emergency surgery to repair a broken hip, pelvis, and tailbone.

Fortunately she recovered and there were no more trips to Mexico after that episode.

I was officially done!

And since that summer, I rejoined the MSBL and continued my passion and quest for 300 with the league.

In life, we strive and we conquer to be the best. All I ever wanted out of my life was to be the best at something. And although I accomplished many things, I lived my life doing something that was very precious and dear to my heart, the game of baseball, where *my passion lives in the core!*

This all brought my family closer in so many ways, to where they lived vicariously through all of my travels, trials and tribulations.

It's the game of baseball—our National Pastime—and it's something beautiful, something with so many lessons to learn, as I did. So for me, it's easy to say that baseball is life.

For an arm that was changed from right to left at an early age, it became a passion that lives so deep in the core, that it has no ending.

Not for me anyway. On May 7 of 2011, I turned 47 with the ball still in my hands, which means I'm still pitching for 300.

HardBall News Alert:

The Next 300 Game Winner?

Many experts say that after Randy Johnson retires, no other pitcher may ever win 300 games in the major leagues. Even less likely was the idea that any MSBL pitcher would ever win 300 games.

Think about it. Ten wins a year would be a good average, and at that pace, it would take a guy 30 years to reach the 300 milestone. Despite the odds, Santa Fe, New Mexico resident **Rod Tafoya** has taken aim at this lofty goal, and he is now more than 70 percent of the way towards his goal. On May 12th, Rod sent us an email to advise that his victory total has reached 219, and that he was planning on reaching the 300 milestone in the year 2013—barring injuries.

Rod currently plays for the Albuquerque Brewers in the New Mexico MSBL. We wish him the best of luck in his quest, and we look forward to reporting his progress from time to time.

LEFT: New Mexico MSBL pitcher Rod Tafoya.

HardBall Magazine   Summer 2008

Just to let you know

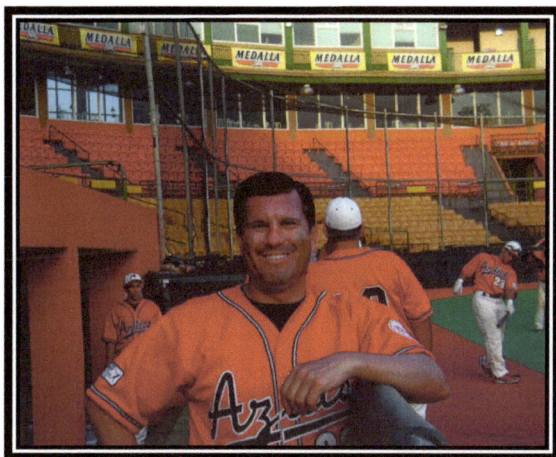

... In high school I wore uniform numbers 30 and 34 in honor of Hall of Famer Nolan Ryan from his years with the Angels and Astros.

Now I wear No. 32 in honor of fellow left-handed Hall of Famer Sandy Koufax, who pitched only for the Dodgers.

... In the minor leagues and in college I wore a black "Rawlings" baseball glove.

Pitching in Mexico, I wore a black "Rolin" baseball glove, a custom model that I purchased at the glove factory in Aquascalientes. It had my name stitched in the leather and proudly displayed the USA and Mexico flags on the backside.

100th win: It was October 28 of 2001, a complete-game 27-7 rout over Sonoma County, Calif., in the MSBL World Series while pitching for the Portland DeMarini Giants. Record now read 100-12 for a .893 winning percentage.

200th win: It was April 29 of 2007, shutting down the Nationals, 15-0, while pitching for the Albuquerque Mets. I went five innings with 10 strikeouts. Record now read 200-27 for a .881 winning percentage.

Photograph Courtesy of Sonya Cogan Photography

250th win: It was July 11 of 2010, an 11-4, 5-inning success over the Cubs while pitching for the Albuquerque Brewers in the MABL. I struck out seven. Record now read 250-38 for a .868 winning percentage.

... More on my late buddy, Albuquerque police officer Germaine Casey. I can never forget the wonderful ways and friendship I shared with him, his experiences in the game of baseball, the knowledge he instilled in me.

Originally from Chicago, Casey was drafted out of high school by the Atlanta Braves, and his connection to the windy city was the reason I got to play for so many Chicago teams: The Reds, the Tomatoes, the Giants, the Legends, the Aztecs, and the Chicago-Brooklyn Royals.

... Ah, the **core**.

Defining the **core** can be as simple as cutting a baseball in half and finding a red rubber ball in the center. Replace the red rubber ball with a heart and you have what makes up the ingredients to my **AGELESS ARM**.

On the flip side, defining the core can be a more complex definition:

It can be much deeper and spiritual.

It comes from passion, which comes from the heart.

It's something you are born with.

It's something that's instilled from your parents.

It's in your DNA.

It's how you are wired inside.

It's in the genes, genetics, and hard work that goes into everything.

It's the spiritual heart.

It's the path of enlightenment.

It's the mind, body, and soul of ones' inner being.

It's the heart or source of matrix where everything arises.

It's the athletic state or being in the flow of art.

I'm certain that the **core** had a beginning further back from when my parents were born. It's defined as the central part of anything. It's the heart or inner-most part.

But my **core** has been around as long as baseball has been played. It's of course the inner part of the white-stitched ball.

It's my *passion!*

Photograph Courtesy of Visual Touch Sports Photography

Index

About the Author

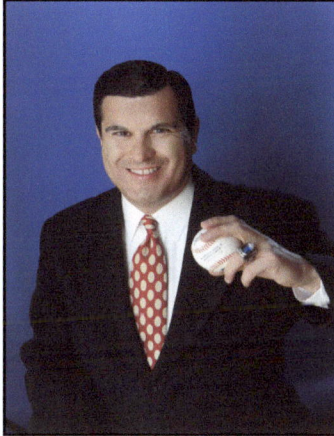

KyleZimmermanPhotography.com

J. Rodney Tafoya – Now the author of his first book – Ageless Arm – baseball has played a huge role in Rod's colorful career, but never secondary to education and family.

Born and raised in Santa Fe, New Mexico, he was the youngest of four brothers and one sister born to Tony and Maude Tafoya. He began his education at Gonzales Elementary School, then entered St. Michael's High School as a seventh-grader. At St. Michael's, he was student body vice president his senior year, enjoyed English most of all, and is presently a foundation board member of his alma mater.

At New Mexico Highlands University in Las Vegas, N.M., Rod majored in business management and studied three years there before transferring to New-man University in Wichita, Kan., and graduating in 1989 with a degree in business management. Not only was he solid in academics, but, as he was back at St. Michael's, Rod continued on as a stellar left-handed pitcher both at NMHU and at Newman. He was hooked on community services and still is. When the struggling nation of Guatemala was in times of need, Rod was right there in 1999-2000 as part of a Rotary International Project to aid the needy. He traveled to Guatemala, also served as an inter-preter, and even offered his assistance when an emergency surgery arose. Still at it, he also contrib-uted to the annual baseball clinic held in Espanola, N.M., and spends most of his free time teaching pitching mechanics to youngsters. Then there's his love for playing baseball and love for his family.

Currently employed as a vice president of Bank of West in Albuquerque, N.M., he credits his late mother and father for instilling a good work ethic, passion, and a will to dream positive for his many successes in life. He is also thankful for his older brother, Jack, for taking the time to help him turn into a classic south-paw pitcher over these remarkable 45 years. Jim, Glenn and Judy are his other siblings who still mar-vel at his achievements on the mound.

VISIT

SPEAKING VOLUMES ONLINE

HUGO, NEBULA,

EDGAR, SHAMUS,

ANTHONY MACAVITY, AGATHA,

CARL SANDBERG, ELLERY QUEEN,

OWEN WISTER, SPUR

&

BRAM STOKER

AWARD-WINNING

USA TODAY & NEW YORK TIMES

BEST-SELLING AUTHORS

www.speakingvolumes.us